Hephzibah

and the

Dragon

Emperor Pu Yi and the Important Documents

REVISED

Karen Roberts

KK Roberts Books

KK Roberts Books US
PO Box 363
Ridgefield, WA 98642
Visit my website: kkrobertsbooks.us

ISBN: Hardback: 979-8-9886431-8-0
Paperback: 979-8-9886431-0-4
eBook: 979-8-9886431-1-1

The Last Emperor

Guangxu Emperor was the tenth emperor of the Qing dynasty. He attempted a constitutional monarchy as part of his Hundred Days' Reform. This reform would have allowed Chinese citizens to vote in an election. The national, cultural, political, and educational reform lasted 103 days. However, this reform abruptly stopped when his mother's older sister, Empress Dowager Cixi, put him under house arrest. During this time, Empress Dowager Cixi ruled in his place. The level of arsenic in Guangxu Emperor's remains was 2,000 times higher than the normal range. Arsenic was the cause of his death, death by poisoning.

Murder was suspected. Laws of succession indicated the new emperor was the paternal great-grandson of Daoguang Emperor. In 1908 when Guangxu Emperor died, Puyi was brought into the rule, even though he was only two years old. Puyi's birth father was alive. However, Puyi was cut off from his birth family for four years. The Empress Dowager Longyu, the widow of Guangxu Emperor, ruled in Puyi's place while he was too young to govern himself.

January 1, 1912

The Republic of China was formally established on January 1, 1912, following the Xinhai Revolution. The revolution resulted from more than ten years of revolts and uprisings.

February 12, 1912

On February 12, 1912, Empress Dowager Longyu agreed to dissolve the monarchy rule on behalf of Emperor Puyi to allow for the establishment of the republic. The Republic of China told her this was what the people wanted. Puyi was six years old at this time. As part of the "Articles of Favorable Treatment of the Ta Qing Emperor after his Abdication," Puyi was allowed to live in the Forbidden City with his 470 eunuchs as a temporary measure.

The Summer Palace was in preparation for Puyi and the royal family. The Republic of China retained Puyi's title. He was allowed the courtesies of foreign monarchs. He was to receive an annual subsidy of $4,000,000. Puyi continued to live in the palace of the Forbidden City in Beijing. However, he no longer ruled over the people of China.

Puyi was not allowed to make his own decisions. He was treated as a child while holding the title of Emperor of China. In March 1922, Puyi was the age of 15 and determined to marry. A marriage would ensure treatment as an adult. The palace administrators presented Puyi with photos of five pre-selected candidates for marriage. He wasn't given the opportunity to meet the candidates. He didn't know who he would like. The selection process lasted for an entire year. His first choice was Wenxiu.

Wenxiu was a princess from the Mongol Erdet Clan. Her grandfather Xi Zhen was the official secretary of the Qing Dynasty. Xi Zhen had six sons and more than 500 houses. Her family was under the Yellow Banner of the Eight Banners of Manchu. The officials lost their rights at Puyi's abdication. The government sold Xi Zhen's houses one after another. He was devastated. He studied Buddhism to find comfort.

Wenxiu's father, Tuan Kung, died when she was young. Her mother and sisters moved to a crowded section of Beijing to rent a house. They only received a small amount of money and some old furniture. They were now an impoverished family. Her uncle Wen Ch'i moved in with them to make it more manageable.

Wenxiu grew up to be a beautiful girl. She was slender, and her face was white and rich. Her uncle took a picture of Wenxiu and sent it to the House of Internal Affairs. He hoped Wenxiu to be chosen for marriage. Wenxiu's personality was quiet, gentle, polite, knowledgeable, and reasonable. Her teachers at the private elementary school loved her. Her Chinese and arithmetic were excellent. She recognized the difficulties her widowed mother faced. In her free time, she helped her mother by doing housework and odd jobs, such as embroidery.

Wenxiu was favored by the high consort Ching Yi but opposed by Duankang, the royal consort. Although Wenxiu was born in Beijing, she had an Outer Mongolian heritage. Regarding the ruling class, "It was better to marry them than to go to war with them," was one view. Puyi was instructed, "You had to take what you could get, and sometimes the woman was not so pretty." Puyi sighed in relief; this girl was pretty.

Duankang vetoed Puyi's selection. Duankang told Puyi, "Wenxiu is impoverished, ugly, and only acceptable as a concubine." The palace administrators told Puyi to select again, now from four candidates. Puyi didn't want each of his choices vetoed, one by one. A veto was heart-wrenching.

Puyi asked the princes, including his father, for guidance. He was encouraged to make a decision. This process was exhausting for all of them. "There should be nothing to this business of selecting a wife. Just put a circle around one of the pictures," encouraged the princes. Puyi put a circle around Wanrong and selected her as his wife and the future empress.

Wanrong was born in Beijing. She was a member of the Manchurian nobility. She was proficient in piano, chess, calligraphy, and painting. Her favorite sport was tennis. Her mother died shortly after she was born. A stepmother raised her. The name Wanrong meant "Graceful as a dragon."

Puyi exercised tradition and his right to take more than one wife. Sir Reginald Fleming Johnston who tutored Puyi in English writes in his book *Twilight in the Forbidden City* that Puyi preferred only to choose one wife.

The dowagers tearfully reproached him to follow the tradition of his ancestors and urged him to select more than one wife.

Puyi writes in his book *From Emperor to Citizen* that high consorts Ching Yi and Jung Hui continued to argue and suggested he choose Wenxiu as a consort rather than allow her to go to one of his subjects. They insisted an emperor must have an empress and a consort. This statement determined his decision. He was eager to fully be an emperor so that he could finally make his own decisions. Puyi chose Wenxiu as his secondary consort.

March 14, 1922

On the front page of March 14, 1922, Court Gazette announced the selection of Wanrong as empress. The Gazette reported the selection of Wenxiu as a secondary consort a few pages in. March 15, 1922, the Herald publicized the betrothal of Puyi and Wanrong. Jung Yuan, Wanrong's father, received the button of the first rank, became an officer of the imperial bodyguard, with the right to access Puyi, and received the privilege of riding on horseback in the Forbidden City. Wenxiu's uncle received the position of state council member of the Ministry of Civil Affairs.

June 4, 1922

On June 4, 1922, before the wedding, Puyi attempted to escape from the Forbidden City. He planned to renounce the title of emperor to the Chinese people with an apology. Sir Johnston rented an additional car at his hotel parking garage, as Puyi requested; however, after an hour of discussion, he did not agree to aid Puyi's escape. Puyi did not want to venture out on his own in the streets of Beijing. He wanted to share a car with Sir Johnston and have a second car for trusted staff. Puyi felt cooped up and wanted out. He felt the title of emperor was a farce. He was an idle pensioner. There was something fundamentally wrong with his present situation. He would not rest until it changed. He wanted to attend Oxford as a student and tour other countries.

October 21, 1922

On October 21, 1922, Puyi's wedding to Princess Wanrong began with betrothal presents. The animals were 18 sheep and two horses. The fabric was 40 pieces of satin and 80 rolls of cloth. The gifts were marched from the Forbidden City to Wanrong's house, accompanied by court musicians and cavalry. Eighteen sheep were herded through the streets of Beijing. The newspaper announced the procession.

On the same day, Puyi sent betrothal presents to Wenxiu's mother. Puyi saw this as a family he could help. Noting the widowed mother rented a house, Puyi bought her a courtyard house and red sandalwood furniture. A courtyard house has a main entrance in the southeast corner, a building on the north side for the first generation in the location that receives the most sun, a structure for the second generation on the east side, a building for relatives who visit on the west side, and a building on the south side near the main entrance for gathering. A large courtyard is in the middle of the four buildings. Puyi then sent gifts identical to those sent to Wanrong's family. The newspaper did not report the gifts Wenxiu received.

November 4, 1922

On November 4, 1922, the marriage contracts were signed. Puyi gave more presents. Wanrong and Wenxiu each received 100 ounces of gold, 10,000 ounces of silver, one gold tea set, two silver tea sets, two silver bowls, 100 pieces of satin, and two horses with saddles and bridles. Their parents received 40 ounces of gold, 4,000 ounces of silver, one gold tea set, one silver tea set, two silver bowls, 40 pieces of satin, 100 rolls of cloth, two horses with saddles and bridles, two suits of court robes, two cases of winter garments, and one girdle of honor. Their siblings each received eight pieces of satin, 16 rolls of cloth, and a writing set.

Two hundred thirty-seven celebrities arrived in Beijing to attend the wedding. The wedding attendees were to enter through the Gate of Spiritual Valor. The former president Hsu Shih-Chang gave twenty-eight pieces of porcelain, a sumptuous Chinese carpet, and $20,000 as a wedding gift. Wenxiu was the first to arrive. It was her responsibility to greet the new empress.

The palace's administrators planned the fixed time for the bride's arrival to be 4:00 a.m. when the waxing gibbous moon is at its fullest. The bride was to be ready to leave her parental home shortly after 3:00 a.m. The court astrologers decided the date and hour of the emperor's wedding. Nothing was decided in the Forbidden City without divination. The middle of the night was not unusual. Manchu weddings are traditionally nocturnal events.

November 30, 1922

Puyi couldn't sleep. Who plans a wedding at such an hour? What a thoughtless thing to do. No one informed him of this nocturnal Manchu custom and both brides are Manchurian. At the stroke of midnight on November 30, Puyi, dressed in a robe, entered the Palace of Heavenly Tranquility. A scepter, symbolizing the supreme power of the emperor, was placed on the table. Alongside it, a gold seal and a gold scroll were presents for the empress. He made his formal declaration to marry Wanrong.

December 1, 1922

He sent honor guards for Wanrong in a Phoenix sedan chair around one o'clock in the morning. The chair was decorated in golden and blue phoenixes and accented with yellow curtains. The yellow curtains were decorated with symbols of good fortune, happiness, and longevity; phoenixes, bats, flowers, and colorful clouds reflected the sunrise. A horse troupe led the military bands. Two military bands performed Western and traditional Chinese music in succession. This music ensured the last sleeping resident was awake for the event.

Wanrong was ready at the appointed hour and entered the sedan chair without hesitation. Wanrong's hair was styled in two buns. She was dressed in a dragon and phoenix robe. A red veil was placed over her face, a crimson and satin cloth embroidered with a dragon and phoenix.

Three thousand people escorted the empress to the imperial palace, along with 72 dragon and phoenix parasols and flags, 30 pairs of imperial lanterns, and various weapons. Tens of thousands of citizens gathered in the streets to view the procession, even though it was three in the morning on December 1, 1922. The full moon that lit the night sky retreated behind a cloud. The sparsely placed electric street lights in Beijing barely penetrated the darkness. Yet, the orderly citizens remained in place to catch the view of Wanrong. Finally, the sedan chair entered the Forbidden City through the Donghua Gate, carried by 22 eunuchs.

According to Chinese and Manchu customs, Puyi did not meet Wanrong until their wedding. Court etiquette also required Puyi to not see the bride before the wedding. So he was not even curious about her appearance until he saw her in her wedding gown. At this time, the red veil continued to hide her face. Yet the marriage commitment was already set into place.

According to Manchu custom, Puyi was to shoot three arrows over his bride to drive away the evil spirits. This tradition may have been the reason for the adornment on her head. Puyi decided not to do this. It was too dangerous to shoot arrows without wearing his eyeglasses. The ceremony was too important for Puyi to wear them. For the foreigners, he read a short speech he had prepared in English. This speech concluded the ceremonies for the guests.

The couple was led to the nuptial chamber in the Palace of Earthly Tranquility, the east warm cabinet decorated in red, the color of love. According to Manchu tradition, the bride stepped over a large fire, a saddle, and an apple. Puyi could have taken away the veil with a measuring scale, warning the bride to be thrifty. However, Puyi took away the red veil that covered her face with his hands and saw his empress for the first time.

The couple had to go through more rituals, including eating dumplings to bring children quickly, longevity noodles to ensure long life, and drinking from the nuptial wine cup. Finally, the public rituals were complete. Puyi left his beautiful bride alone on the bed without saying a word. He was gone for the whole night. Wanrong quietly waited for his arrival.

Rumors spread, "The 17-year-old Puyi, dazzled by the red decorations all around him, panicked and fled from the wedding chamber." According to Puyi's autobiography, he felt stifled. Everything was red. It looked like a melted red wax candle. Wanrong bowed her head low. Everything done or said up to that point was a carefully scripted ritual. He did not know whether to stand or sit. Finally, he decided he preferred his residence. He returned to the Hall of the Nurture of the Mind.

Puyi married Wenxiu the same night in a separate ceremony, and she became his Secondary Consort. Puyi was 16 years of age, soon to be 17. Wenxiu was 13 years old to some reports.

The math calculation shows Wenxiu was only 12. Puyi's autobiography states Wenxiu was "not yet 14" and at age 12, one year earlier during the selection. The discrepancy is because, at the beginning of the selection process, Wenxiu was 11 going on 12 and advertised as 12 by her uncle. At the marriage, she was 12 going on 13. Puyi thought she was 13 going on 14 at the time of marriage. Puyi never did the math.

Wenxiu knelt three times and bowed down three times, touching her head to the ground, a grand kowtow or nine-fold prostration. She practiced this many times since arriving at the Forbidden City. She hoped Puyi would be pleased.

After the wedding ceremony, Puyi told Wenxiu, "Go down and rest." Puyi was attempting to be considerate. He was tired. He hadn't slept all night. Wenxiu was the first to arrive for the wedding ceremonies that evening. He assumed she was tired and needed rest.

Wenxiu interpreted Puyi's request as indifference towards her. It gave her a feeling of uncertainty.

Later that night, Puyi joined Wanrong and Wenxiu in the Palace of Earthly Tranquility. Wanrong was 16 years old and had a better idea of what to expect on a wedding night. She was a virgin too, but she recognized Puyi as a 16-year-old boy, so she took the role of putting Puyi at ease. His response consummated the marriage.

It was Wenxiu's wedding night, too. Puyi felt he had to make it up to her, so he consummated the marriage with Wenxiu instead of waiting. He knew she wasn't yet 14, but he hadn't considered how a girl her age would feel.

The situation shamed Wenxiu, who was not yet 13. To Wenxiu, this wedding night was a weird ménage à trois.

The court astrologers used divination to select the time and date of the wedding. The date was chosen by studying the position of the stars and the moon and selecting the best time for conception. We might think the stars were lying. It was a half-truth. The stars kept their secret and proudly twinkled at their success.

Hephzibah

The night sky keeps its secrets, waiting for the dawn of light to reveal them, when our eyes are ready to be open. Some of the names have been changed.

Hephzibah was a small girl with dark brown hair and nearly black eyes. Her family lived in a small two-bedroom house on Main Street. Hephzibah's mother and father shared one bedroom, her two older sisters shared the second bedroom, and Hephzibah slept in the laundry room. Her pine crib was decorated with pictures in soft pastel green and gold. A mobile hung over the top. The laundry room received good ventilation inside the enclosed back porch. But this was a less than ideal sleeping spot especially when the washing machine was off balance and rocking violently. Her mother would dash from the kitchen to the porch to rescue Hephzibah's crib before it tipped over onto the floor.

Hephzibah's mother was exasperated, "The laundry always smells like cigarette smoke, no matter how many times I wash." She complained, "Opening the laundry room window doesn't help for more than a moment." Repeated attempts to remove the cigarette smoke smell from the clothing added to her long cleaning list.

Hephzibah's father went outside through the front door to smoke. A cigarette after work calmed him after the hectic workday. Hephzibah's father worked fourteen-hour days repairing cars. He needed relaxation when he returned home. He could see that his wife was stressed. He tried to think of ways to help her. Unfortunately, smoking outside didn't seem to stop the smell. Cigarette smoke was in his clothes, even right after a wash.

Getting the children ready for bed was an accomplishment. As a result, it caused discord that Hephzibah would scream at night just when everyone had fallen asleep. The scream was loud, sudden, and high-pitched.

Hephzibah's mother reasoned that she had a fear of monsters. She said to Hephzibah, "I did everything I could to get you to be quiet." She took a flashlight, got down on her hands and knees, waved the flashlight back and forth under the crib, and showed her no monsters were hiding there.

Hephzibah's mother purchased a cute night light. "I bought this just for you. Don't you want a night light?" Hephzibah's mother asked her. "It is a cute Bugs Bunny one. You like Bugs Bunny. Don't you?" she prodded. Bugs Bunny was Hephzibah's favorite cartoon.

Hephzibah was nearly in tears. Her mother didn't understand. Bugs Bunny was her favorite cartoon. That was true. But Bugs Bunny shining in the dark would not stop the monster. Bugs Bunny had clever tricks. He was able to get himself out of a jam, not defend someone else. "Can I have an Elmer Fudd night light?" Hephzibah asked.

"What kind of girl wants Elmer Fudd?" her mother asked, with a tone of disgust. She didn't consider there might be a reason for the screams.

The night light made it easier for the monster. There was no warning light before he came. "I don't want light," Hephzibah said the next night. She shook her head in defiance. "I want the dark. I want it completely dark," she insisted.

"Not even a little light? Do you want pitch-black darkness? Aren't you afraid of the dark?" Her mother asked. She paused and said softly, "Usually, children are afraid of monsters hiding in the dark."

"No, the dark is peaceful," Hephzibah answered. "The monster can't find me in the dark." The dark was her only defense. Her crib acted as a cage and prevented her escape. The rest of the family was safely inside the house. So she was the only one trapped outside.

"Well, I suppose that makes sense," her mother replied. She turned the night light off at the switch. "The night light is here if you need it," she said gently.

When Hephzibah's mother found cigarette burns on Hephzibah's head, she couldn't think of when she was around cigarettes. She asked her husband about the burns. He didn't say anything. He was in deep thought. So she started to suspect her husband. "Why must he smoke?" she asked herself.

At night Hephzibah's father checked the back door lock. Then, he switched to smoking a tobacco pipe. Now her father could smoke in the house on a rainy day. The tobacco pipe smoke didn't bother his wife as much. It wasn't the smell that lingered in the laundry.

Hephzibah's mother was afraid of Child Protective Services (CPS). She put Hephzibah's hair up in a ponytail at the top of her head to hide the burns.

Hephzibah's older sisters teased her. "Your hair looks like a whale spout," they mocked. Hephzibah cried. Her mother insisted on the hairstyle.

"Would you like to wear a hat instead?" Hephzibah's mother asked. The hat was okay. It was white and shaped to fit snugly on her head. At least she didn't look like a whale. She secured the white hat around her chin. Her mother insisted it had to stay on all day while indoors at the preschool to hide her burns.

Hephzibah's preschool teacher became concerned. Hephzibah refused to take off the hat all day. The teacher talked to her mother about it. At home, Hephzibah had to stay indoors instead of going outside to play with the neighborhood children. Her mother was afraid the neighbors might call CPS. Her sisters were allowed to play with their friends.

Hephzibah was learning the wrong things. She was learning to hide her injuries. Hephzibah was learning not to report predators. She was learning to keep silent when she was in pain. Her pain tolerance was increasing. Hephzibah climbed out of her crib and slept underneath it on the cold, hard floor. She felt safe there. She fell asleep without worrying about what might come.

Hephzibah's mother was learning to ignore her daughter when she cried for help. She perceived climbing out of the crib as naughty. She told Hephzibah to stay in her crib. Hephzibah willfully disobeyed. It is hard for people to reframe information later.

The laundry room was also the back porch. The back porch side window was above Hephzibah's crib. Each night Hephzibah's father made sure the back door was locked. However, her parents didn't lock the window of the back porch. Hephzibah's mother used the window for ventilation when she did laundry.

The unlocked window gave a neighbor a chance to come by with his flashlight. He would inch open the window, reach through with his arm, and extinguish his cigarette on the top of Hephzibah's head. Her screams weren't night terrors or fear of monsters. Her screams were from the pain of the burns. Hephzibah's monster was real.

The family moved to a larger house in the country. The move was her father's solution for the sleeping situation. He suspected the neighbor was doing something. He didn't know what or how. So he made a deal with his in-laws to raise the male Holsteins born on the dairy. He would raise them for beef as side work to repairing cars. Now the family had farm chores to do and animals to care for. They also had a half-acre garden to plant and water.

Opa and Oma

At every opportunity, Hephzibah would stay with Opa and Oma. It was at her grandparents' house that she learned how to walk. She was born with deformed feet. She learned to walk alongside her grandparents' golden lab, Casey. At first, she imitated walking on four legs. Her legs moved better than her arms which became sore. Then she moved faster, walking on two feet. Finally, her reward was catching up to Casey. She put her arms around the yellow fur on his neck to give him a hug.

Opa had salt-and-pepper gray hair. He would nap on the sofa. Hephzibah would put a single penny on his closed eyelids and try to get away before he could wake up and grab her. Each time he managed to catch her, she yelled, "Oh no!" and he would laugh. But he never gave her beatings.

"Some people eat to live," Oma said, "I live to eat." Her tummy was round to prove it. Hephzibah helped Oma prepare food in the kitchen. Oma liked food that was spicy and had plenty of flavors. Hephzibah learned to like hot peppers to please Oma. "I used to be thin," Oma explained. "My father would invite everyone in town. He would clear the furniture out of the house and stack it in the yard. Then we would dance on the hardwood floor in the living room." "What do you want to be when you grow up?" Oma asked Hephzibah.

"I want to be a princess," Hephzibah responded. Every girl her age had this dream. She imagined the princess's life would be peaceful. "I'll have parties, invite everyone in town, and dance on the living room floor," Hephzibah decided. "The way your family did in Nebraska," she said as she beamed at Oma.

"A princess who puts pennies on people's eyes," Oma shook her head. "Being a princess is a huge responsibility," Oma explained. "Many brides were married to a ruler to stop a conflict between countries. The princess might not even know the man or what he looks like. But it was her job to keep the peace." Oma looked at Opa sleeping on the sofa and smiled, "But there are many princesses in the family."

Hephzibah took her comment to mean Oma might have become a princess but was stuck with Opa. Hephzibah hugged Oma in sympathy and went outside to play in the yard with Casey. It was a large yard. Half of the yard was a vegetable garden with green beans and corn. The other half was a grassy area dedicated to the horseshoe and Frisbee games. These were games Opa had mastered. A large Bing cherry tree grew on the south side of the house. Oma lived by the phrase, "I would rather be gardening." The beauty of this choice showed all around in the foliage.

If Hephzibah stayed for a week, Opa would invite her to help him light the candles. First, he would light a candle with a match. Then she would light another candle using the same flame. Next, he would say a small prayer in German. Then they would watch the candle flames dance. Hephzibah would look forward to this, "Can we light the candles?" she asked Opa.

"No," Opa answered. "That is only on Friday nights. It's not time yet," Opa instructed, "I'll tell you when it's time." So, they lit the candles at nightfall and watched the metal angels dance in circles from the heat.

Oma had no problems with Hephzibah. She helped when Oma asked. Oma could not understand why her mother complained. While Hephzibah stayed with them, Opa received a video from his cousin. Opa's cousins sold the Kansas mansion along with the artwork on the walls and pictures of their grandfather. A local judge purchased the estate from the family. The money from the sale went towards medical bills for a granddaughter who was born severely disabled.

The mansion had a main staircase and a separate staircase for the servants. The master bedroom had a walk-in closet. The estate also had a "Marilyn Monroe room" filled with collectibles and memorabilia from Marilyn

Monroe. Opa asked his cousin, "Why didn't you sell the Marilyn Monroe collectibles instead of the entire mansion?"

His cousin replied, "Oh, those were the first to go."

Oma looked sorrowful, "It makes you wonder if they understood the value of what they were given. Their grandparents entrusted it to them because they thought they would take care of it." But instead, the mansion was run-down and needed repairs when it was sold it.

Hephzibah realized the royalty was on Opa's side of the family. She had misjudged him and knelt next to the sofa. She adjusted her skirt to cover her legs. "Oh, that was your family," Hephzibah gasped to Opa. She always assumed it was Oma's family. She said, "I'm sorry, Opa. I didn't know."

"It was alright," Opa assured her. "My father was a black sheep. He decided he liked the German women better," he said this and winked at Oma. Oma's ancestors were from Luxemburg.

Oma interjected, "His father had married the family servant. Grandfather cut him out of the Will. He said he liked her so much he had to marry her," Oma explained. "It was the right thing to do. She came from Germany at the start of World War I. She immigrated to England first and learned the language. She must have been sponsored by someone in England and recommended to arrive at a mansion in Kansas. We don't know much about her. She told stories about her family in the kitchen while we prepared dinner. She was the oldest daughter with many younger brothers." Oma added with a smile, "Now you have a way to find her one day."

Youlin

There was a shift in the royal class from the Manchurian to the Han ethnic majority. The Manchurians were seen as traitors after WWII, as sympathizers to Japan. Youlin's mother was Han Chinese, the ethnic majority. But his father was Manchurian and from the old regime.

Jin Youlin grew up in a tall apartment complex in Beijing. The family's living space was a single room with a small kitchen area to prepare food. He was the only child and would remain so. In 1980 China enacted the one-child policy making it illegal to have two children. So, it was the family's great luck that they had a boy to carry on the family name. They raised him in the Tao religion of his father until the age of two.

[The book on Tao is missing!]

December 4, 1982

On December 4, 1982, China adopted the Constitution of the People's Republic of China. The Constitution was the supreme law. It was now illegal to teach religion to children under 18. Teaching religion to children would result in the loss of parental rights. Jin Youzhi, Youlin's father, feared the government. He did not want to lose his parental rights and custody of his son. His son meant everything to him, so he complied with the law. Youzhi taught Youlin Tao as a philosophy instead of as a religion. Instead of teaching him to pray, Youzhi taught him to hope.

Both Youlin's mother and father worked to make ends meet. They poured everything into providing what they could for their son. Unfortunately, they couldn't afford the best education. Instead, they taught their son the languages of the region, Manchu, Cantonese, and the foreign languages of neighboring countries. These were the same languages Youzhi learned when he was growing up. This skill allowed Youlin to "talk shop" with people in their native language.

April 15, 1989

On April 15, 1989, Hu Yaobang, a former Communist Party General Secretary, died. During his time in office, Hu tried to rehabilitate the people persecuted during the Cultural Revolution. In addition, he attempted to bring democratic reform to China. There was a gathering of 200,000 students in Tiananmen Square starting on April 22, 1989, during Hu's funeral ceremony. They gathered to mourn Hu Yaobang's death. Pro-democracy student protests began and continued growing for several weeks. They gathered without a permit.

June 4, 1989

On June 4, 1989, there was an overwhelming victory election in Poland, resulting in a collapse of communism in Eastern Europe. This event was an icy moment for communist leaders. That same day, China called martial law to halt the student protest. The People's Liberation Army massacred student demonstrators. In the aftermath of the Tiananmen Square massacre, US Congress imposed economic sanctions, resulting in a downturn in China's economy.

This massacre was in Beijing, the hometown of Youzhi and his family. Youlin was in elementary school at the time. It had a profound effect to see so many who tried to bring political change brought to a brutal end. Youlin explained, "This wasn't an attack on the poor. Many good, educated people were lost. Not everyone was educated at that time. They were from up-standing families. But this made no difference."

This attack wasn't just a report in the Beijing newspaper or on television. Youlin saw it with his own eyes. He experienced it. His mouth shifted to the right, and the right corner of his upper lip turned into a curl as he remembered seeing the blood. Youlin's face and mouth twisted into a grimace, "The blood didn't just drip down the streets but," he paused, "flowed down the streets."

A stench filled the air in Beijing. Mangled lifeless bodies were piled high. "The bodies lingered for three days," Youlin recalled. "But then they cleaned it up," he nodded and smiled in relief. A natural fear remained, or an instilled respect. His hope for the future became firmer. It had to.

BS in Engineering

Youzhi didn't want Youlin to parade around. He wanted him to be humble. Youzhi put Youlin through college to earn a Bachelor of Science in Engineering in China. He wanted him to concentrate on becoming an engineer. Youlin succeeded well in his studies. He wanted his father and mother to be proud of him.

Youlin found his mechanical engineering specialty area in Thermodynamics, exploring the transfer of heat and the science of large numbers. He designed for Huawei Technologies and obtained a patent in 2007. However, he did not feel like he contributed much to the project. The group completed the work as a team. The company insisted on including his name on the patent.

Probability indicated there would be as many girls as boys born in China, so it should be a one to one (1:1) relationship. Despite probability, the one-child policy had led to boys outnumbering girls in China by seven to one (7:1), so marriage was delayed for Youlin. Dating was hard to come by. China prized virginity.

Youzhi encouraged Youlin to go to the United States to find a woman suitable for him. "We love you, son," Youzhi said in a gravel voice, "We'll accept whoever you choose. Just bring her home." Youzhi had seen his son complete his engineering degree and start a career as an engineer. But now he was getting up in years. He wanted nothing more than to see his son married and have a child.

The University of California Irvine accepted Youlin to graduate school. The graduate school is prestigious, and difficult to gain admission. That in itself was an accomplishment. Youlin earned his Master of Science degree in Thermodynamics. In 2012 and 2013, he continued to obtain patents designing for the United States branch of Huawei Technologies.

Youlin reached his goal of earning a Master of Science degree. His goal of finding a suitable wife was not completed. His selection process was thorough. He carefully examined every aspect and considered them, from finances to political views to entertainment to favorite foods to religion to genealogy. He was becoming too old to be a virgin. He was starting to form habits that a woman would not appreciate. However, instead of relaxing his criteria, it became more selective.

Hephzibah

Hephzibah visited her boyfriend, David, to break off the relationship. The visit was following his birthday and Valentine's Day. The timing was poor. David wanted her to drink half a bottle of wine. She insisted on the doctor's recommended half a glass. He was angry at her lack of cooperation. He drank the rest of the bottle. She left in frustration. But not before he got her pregnant.

David had a vasectomy while in the Navy. The Navy doctor tied knots in the vas deferens. The Navy teaches many knots, but this knot didn't stay tied. David thought he was shooting blanks.

Hephzibah's relationship with David was over and done. Her history of miscarriages kept her silent. It would be better if people didn't know. She didn't want to start that conversation and have uncomfortable questions to follow. "What happened?" and "Oh, so sad." She was not expecting the pregnancy to last the full term.

ISIS Came into Power

At the same time, ISIS came into power in the Middle East. First, it started small. Some Muslims were excited about the prospect of conquering Israel for Palestine. But over time, many changed their minds and stood with signs that said, "Not My Muslim." They did not want to be associated with the violence of ISIS. This hatred wasn't what their religion was about. The Quran forbids violence. Even worse, ISIS purified the religion by killing other Muslims. In total more Muslims were murdered by ISIS than any other religious group.

Hephzibah had not taken any particular stand until Felicia, a friend who lived in Kuwait, contacted with horrific news, "The scumbags are at my doorstep."

It first started with fraudulent banknotes. ISIS had forged banknotes stating to be from the Bank of Kuwait. Kuwait quickly prosecuted the fraud. But what was to be said then about the banknotes from the Bank of Syria? ISIS claimed to be well funded by the Bank of Syria. Wouldn't those banknotes be fraudulent too?

Hephzibah's suspicions turned out to be true. The Bank of Syria went bankrupt. The Syria bank notes were fraudulent too. Fraud was how his war was funded, first with fraudulent banknotes and then by taking places of value, such as oil fields, with military force. How would anyone stop a man who does this?

Then ISIS eliminated minor Muslim factions to purify the Islam religion. An ISIS fighter bombed a mosque in Kuwait as the men were kneeling to pray. You don't need to be a Muslim to be offended by that. On its own, that had Hephzibah designing a weapon. "I'm willing to take on a thousand ISIS with rifles," she said, "Single-handed, if necessary." She was so angry.

Hoping on an airplane to Kuwait was not the best idea. Not just because she wanted to take on one thousand rifles, but because of her medical condition. She couldn't fly.

Medical Trouble

Hephzibah's primary doctor was the one who trained the medical students at Oregon Health & Sciences University, OHSU. He would come into her exam room with two or three medical students. They made good observations and then left together.

Occasionally her primary doctor left for Africa to work as a surgeon. At these times, she was scheduled with the nurse practitioner. When Hephzibah's primary doctor retired, the clinic transferred her primary care to the nurse practitioner. From the clinic's perspective, this made sense for "continuous care."

But it meant Hephzibah could no longer see a doctor, only the nurse. And a doctor could no longer see Hephzibah. If she made an appointment at the front desk, the appointment was changed in back by switching patient files. And there were problems a nurse practitioner wouldn't catch. For example, her comprehensive blood and urine analysis showed she was starving. Her arms, legs, and thighs were thin. Only her belly was distended. The nurse practitioner dismissed these critical clues.

Darius

Hephzibah and Darius were talking and waiting for lab students to arrive. Darius was 5'11" tall and had an athletic build. His skin was the color of walnut butter. He had dark brown curly hair piled on top of his head, very dark eyes, and a warm smile. His job was to help students in the lab. He told her they could accommodate her if the pressure differential in the clean room bothered her too much.

They were waiting to give tours of their research, and they began to chat. Hephzibah looked over her shoulder at his face. "I'm the third girl when my parents were trying for a boy," Hephzibah admitted in a matter-of-fact tone. "My parents already decided their baby's name would be Clancy." She was the third child in a line of daughters, and each time they tried for a boy. "My parents had to scramble for a girl's name."

Hephzibah listened to Darius' story and gasped, "You're a Jew!"

Darius clarified, "Jews are descendants of Judah, which is to the south. I'm an Israelite." Hephzibah had offended him. "My people were exiled to Iran. We were from the ten lost tribes to the north." Darius mentioned literature from his culture. "I'd like to be one of the 144000," he confessed. Now he was referring to Revelation.

Hephzibah pointed out, "To do that, you'd have to be a virgin." She looked at him thoughtfully, "Would it be worth it?"

Darius looked down and started to reconsider.

Darius thought of literature that described Hephzibah. He thought she would be the mother of one who would help the tribes in exile. Not with this pregnancy, maybe another later. "I can't find the books in English," he said. They are in Hebrew, Arabic, and German."

Hephzibah didn't know any of those languages. She asked Darius, "Which of those languages do you speak the most?" She ignored his comment about becoming a mother. Miscarriages had become a norm for her. Giving birth was a lost cause. Giving birth to someone who would help the exiled was improbable.

"I speak Arabic the most," Darius replied. "It's the language of my country." He shrugged.

"Do you know how to fight at all?" Darius asked. He wasn't expecting much, but he bit at the corner of his lips and looked worried.

"I have a first-degree brown belt in karate," Hephzibah replied to Darius. "I was grouped in with the black belts for a sparring tournament, and I won first place in women's black belt sparring. My martial arts opponent decided to forfeit." The buff sparring opponent had recently tested for her black belt and passed the test. However, the opponent decided she would rather sit at a baseball game with her friend and eat hot dogs than spar in the tournament, and she approached the judge's table to withdraw her name.

At first, Hephzibah took this as rejection. Her opponent's absence was regarded as a statement that she wasn't good enough to bother fighting. She kept the metal. Over time, she learned to take pride in winning. She didn't run from the fight.

Darius looked relieved and pleased. "This is better than I thought." He didn't say why it was important to him.

Expelled

The university noticed Hephzibah's growing belly. They didn't voice their accusations directly to her. Instead, they regarded her "weight gain" as "parading a pregnancy." Hephzibah did not want to name the father, especially for a pregnancy she was sure would end in miscarriage. As a result, the university thought she was accusing her math professors of being the father.

The university expected a written response from Hephzibah, but she didn't know what she was responding to. All her focus and energy went into defending her master's thesis. Her advisor told her that nothing else was more important.

After the thesis was complete, there were no answers to her questions. The university received an anonymous file that was designed to cause trouble. The anonymous source instructed, "For best results, involve the mother." The university emailed the information to her mother as an attachment. Hephzibah was too old for the university to contact her mother, and she had never provided permission for the contact.

[Anonymous file was clue #2. The missing book on Tao was clue #1.]

Hephzibah's mother was offended by the request for little tasks in the email and refused to relay messages. The university never obtained permission to involve her, and she felt this communication was the responsibility of the university. She deleted the email.

The university accused Hephzibah of religious discrimination against Muslims. Darius intervened on Hephzibah's behalf at the university. "I didn't mean to offend a Jew," they said. Darius was about to correct them to tell them he was an Israelite, not a Jew. But in exasperation, he let it slide.

Outside the university library Mohammad, a classmate in Mechanical Engineering, prayed with Hephzibah for a resolution. He also prayed that a Muslim would deliver her baby. Then he gave her a gentle hug. People pray for strange things. But God answered his prayers.

Planned Parenthood identified the problem and insisted on a biopsy. The doctor who diagnosed Hephzibah's pregnancy was gynecologist Dr. Homayoun Akhavan-Saraf, MD, but it was too late for live birth.

Her body was returning to normal. A biopsy of the "mass" showed no cancer. It was too large to be a fibroid or two fibroids grown together. On the ultrasound image, the shape of the mass or masses looked like a body and a head. The endocrine lab results, blood analysis, and urine analysis with the other factors and measurements indicated a pregnancy. Hephzibah's pregnancy was far enough along to be diagnosed as a stillbirth.

Wenxiu

Wenxiu lived in the Changchun Palace (Palace of Long Spring-time). Empress Dowager Cixi had lived in this palace for 23 years, so, of course, it was magnificent. Puyi visited Wenxiu once a month at her palace to sit and chat with her. He did not dare see her more often. Wenxiu was pregnant. Puyi's position was uncertain; he did not know what would happen. He knew governments were unstable; they came and went. Generals shifted loyalty. He also assumed he would father more children and at least one with Wanrong, so he confined Wenxiu to the Changchun Palace to protect her from being seen.

The Changchun Palace was deserted. Wenxiu had fewer visitors than Wanrong. Everyone wanted to visit the empress. Wenxiu ate her meals alone. The library in the West Side Hall of the palace became the most frequent place for Wenxiu. She liked to read. So she stayed there all day. Books on the Xipei Temple (a Tibetan temple in Beijing) became a spiritual stronghold. Her mother had not visited her in months. Her mother remarried and was starting a new blended family. Her uncle spent his time at the Ministry of Civil Affairs.

At night her candle was her companion. Wenxiu writes in her diary, "There was a generator in the palace, but it often broke down and it was common to have power failure. Puyi didn't live with his Empress or his Consort, so I had to live alone in the spacious Changchun Palace. The nights were so long and so horrible, and the loneliness in my heart was hard to be got rid of. I lit a candle and faced the lonely lamp, waiting until the candle was burned most. ... A spell of indescribable mawkishness ran through me, and I thought: I was just like this half-burned candle whose tears would run out soon and whose life would be turned into a smoke. Was this place really a palace of magnificence? Maybe it was just a macabre grave!" *Forgotten Lives*

The Summer Palace

Puyi learned to drive a car. Wanrong joined him on a drive to the Summer Palace. The palace's administrators nervously allowed the outing. The republic was preparing the Summer Palace as a permanent residence for them. This trip was an opportunity to provide their approval.

Puyi selected a building to live in.

Wanrong chose her building to live in.

Sir Johnston chose a building and then changed his mind and decided again on one with more access. (Sir Johnston selected two buildings before Wenxiu had a chance to choose one.)

At last, Puyi picked a building for Wenxiu. Puyi approved the living quarters of their future home. Puyi and Wanrong returned to the Forbidden City, hopeful of the future.

Too Much Opium

Puyi visited Wanrong in her palace. After some time, Wanrong became more challenging to handle. The eunuchs noticed Puyi became angry after each visit with Wanrong. Wanrong complained Puyi would transfer Wenxiu's bad mood onto her. Puyi suggested opium to calm Wanrong. Unfortunately, his directive was a mistake.

The eunuchs supplied an unhealthy amount of opium. Wenxiu believed the drug was responsible for Wanrong's infertility. One day, when she saw Wanrong smoking, she said, "Why should you take opium? It would be better to stab at your belly." Wenxiu kept a healthy lifestyle.

Convex Lens Photography

Wenxiu felt fat and ugly. She was retaining water. Her slim figure was gone. Puyi wanted Wenxiu to understand that he found her beautiful, so he used his new camera to take pictures of her. He decided natural lighting would be best, so he brought her out into the courtyard for sunlight in the early morning.

Wenxiu and Puyi played with his new camera, using convex and concave lenses. While using the convex lens they made funny faces and laughed. The photos focused on Wenxiu's face. Her dress and her arms hid her young, thirteen-year-old pregnant figure. The visual distortion of the convex lens obscured her weight gain.

Palace of Established Happiness

Sir Johnston noticed an antique shop had sprung up in his neighborhood. Statues were pawned for their weight in gold instead of their appraised value. At the request of his tutor, Puyi initiated an inquiry at the palace regarding items missing from the treasury. An audit was done on the storeroom of the Place of Established Happiness. This record was the first of a series of audits. The theft was so bad; all of the pearls and jades in Wanrong's crown were replaced with fakes as soon as the wedding ceremony was over.

June 27, 1923

Before another audit could be completed, on June 27, 1923, a fire started in the storeroom.

Wenxiu smelled smoke. She awoke and waved a hand fan in front of her face to stir the air. She felt a wind in the coldness of the night, bringing a warm breeze. The warm breeze was pleasant at first but intuitively wrong. This wasn't the right time of day for a warm wind. Wenxiu heard a commotion. There were panicked yells and shouts and the sound of racing footsteps back and forth in the courtyard. She saw the billowing black cloud of ash blowing to the north in the direction of her palace. In the shadows, the eunuchs raced past her window with buckets of water, large buckets filled full with water carried by two eunuchs, one on each side.

Wenxiu heard the crackling of the fire, the crashing of large pieces of wood, the collapse of a roof landing on a section of the fire, briefly putting part of the fire out, and a deafening moment of silence. And then more raging fires fueling up again. She heard more panicked yells and more racing footsteps. She did not know what was on fire. The eunuchs were carrying buckets of water in the general direction of Puyi's residence. Chinese firefighters came to assist, but at some point, the heat was so bad they could only stand and watch. Foreigners entered the Forbidden City in the night to watch. One foreigner hit a Chinese fireman on the nose with her fan so hard it made his nose bleed. Wenxiu was fearful and didn't know what to do. She was afraid for her safety, the safety of her baby, and the safety of the baby's father. She obediently remained in seclusion, waiting for Puyi.

Puyi strictly told the eunuchs and staff not to enter the Changchun Palace. The eunuchs debated outside Wenxiu's window, "Should we go in to rescue her?" they asked. Others responded, "Under no circumstances are we allowed to enter Wenxiu's residence." The eunuchs sneered, "Even with this fire, the hermit can't be bothered to come out." At the end of the debate, they decided to leave her.

Wenxiu overheard their sneer. "Why are they so disrespectful? Has Puyi died? Is that the reason for the panic? Is that why he hadn't come?" Her emotions were already raging from the seventh month of pregnancy. Tears fell down her face as she imaged her life as a single mother at 13, her baby growing up without a father, and the hardships they would face. The difficulties she and her mother faced when her father died. The extra responsibilities she took on. She quietly sobbed. The soot in the air made her eyes sting and water. Her tears relieved the sting.

The storeroom of the Palace of Established Happiness and everything around it burned to the ground. The Palace of Established Happiness is where most of the Qing treasures were stored. Puyi and Wanrong stood on the pile of ashes inspecting the ruins. The ashes contained bits of gold and silver. It became difficult to know what was burned and what had been sold on the black market. Another kerosene-soaked wad of cotton and wool was placed in the East Hall of the Nurture of the Mind, Puyi's residence. The fire was quickly extinguished. However, this affirmed Puyi's suspicion of arson.

West Side Hall

Puyi went to tell Wenxiu what happened. He did not need to look for her. He knew where she would be. She was awake and frightened, waiting for him in the West Side Hall of the Changchun Palace. Puyi stepped through the door and realized the sight they would see, a very pregnant Wenxiu. She was relieved that Puyi was alive. She had to touch him to make sure. She ran to him sobbing, wrapped her arms around him, and held him tight.

He had not expected her to be worried about him. He only thought about the fire. He wished he had come earlier. Puyi consoled her. He explained the eunuchs would be dismissed and assured her caretakers would remain.

The visit, he expected to be about fifteen minutes, lasted for a couple of hours. When he emerged from her palace, the eunuchs looked at him with raised eyebrows. He was spending time with his wife. He knew they would not have this reaction toward time spent with Wanrong. This did nothing to calm his anger.

Approximately 420 eunuchs were discharged. Fifty trusted eunuchs were kept to care for them and the palace. Where the charred remains of the Palace of Established Happiness once stood, a tennis court was built, Wanrong's favorite sport.

Birth of a Son

Wenxiu had a son. He received the surname Jin, which means gold. Wenxiu was only a child herself and not in a position to raise him. Puyi could see that he married her too young, so the infant was taken outside of the palace by her lady-in-waiting to be raised by servants in Beijing.

A lady-in-waiting works in the Forbidden City but resides outside of the Forbidden City. The lady-in-waiting's own family cared for Jin Youzhi. The lady-in-waiting's family was contracted to raise the child in the Tao religion and to teach him the languages of the region.

Youzhi was also the name Prince Chun gave to Puren, who was four years old when Puyi's son was born. Maybe it was positive intent. Maybe Prince Chun was planning to blend Puyi's son into his family, and he was making that more manageable by having some of his children adopt the Jin surname. Maybe that was the reason he changed Puren's name to Jin

Youzhi. Or perhaps he wanted Puyi to always have a Jin Youzhi with him. Maybe Puyi wanted a son named after his courtesy name.

I believe the reason was that Puyi could receive information about his son and would only need to ask "One or two" to know if the message was about his son or Puren. People who overheard the messenger would naturally assume Puyi was hearing about his half-brother. Messages about his family were always his favorite.

Tang Shixia

In 1924 Pujie, Puyi's younger half-brother, married Tang Shixia of the Tatara clan. Pujie was 17 years old. Tang Shixia was 20.

After this, Wenxiu was encouraged to enjoy fresh air and exercise in the Imperial Garden along with Tang Shixia and Wanrong. They noticed she gained weight during isolation. Wenxiu learned tennis to play with Wanrong and Tang Shixia. Wenxiu was now 14 years old.

September 1924

Events outside of Beijing were about to impact those within. In September 1924, two military leaders in central China quarreled. The quarrel escalated into a civil war. It was clear the situation could not be contained to central China. Wu P'ei-fu camped with his army in Beijing while preparing to invade Manchu. This created anxiety in Beijing and the Forbidden City. Wu P'ei-fu entrusted General Feng Yuxiang with the responsibility of holding the northern passes against flanking of the opposing army.

However, rather than marching ahead to hold off the opposing army, Feng abandoned both the mission and his military leader and returned to Beijing. In the dark hours of the morning on October 23, 1924, Feng Yuxiang came into power in Beijing, China.

The telephones, the telegraphs, and the railway stopped working. By the time the president awoke, troops were stationed outside, and he had no avenue of escape. The citizens of Beijing were unsure of what had happened and panicked. The streets were oddly silent and vacant of pedestrians.

Puyi was unaware of the capture of Beijing but noticed the troops stationed on Prospect Hill. Puyi's eunuch Shao Ying insisted, "We must treat them as our guests."

Puyi countered, "They are there without permission. And I don't know what they intend to do." Ignoring Puyi's protests, Shao Ying sent them tea and food. "Did the troops thank you for the food?" Puyi asked.

"No, and they asked for more," the Shao Ying replied.

Puyi climbed on top of the roof to view the scene with field glasses. Prospect Hill was crowded with soldiers. He wondered, "What were they doing there?"

Puyi's eunuch reported news from outside the walls of the Forbidden City. Sun Yueh, an ally of Feng, led the troops who occupied Prospect Hill. The report Puyi received stated, "Criminals were released from prison. Students were distributing Communist leaflets in the streets." In the next few days, the presidential treasurer was executed. The parliament was dissolved. Wu P'ei-fu was dismissed from his military posts, and the civil war was ordered to cease. A new cabinet was appointed.

October 17, 1924

On October 17, 1924, Sir Johnston visited Cherry Glen, his mountain retreat. He included a mission to scout out the Summer Palace. His trip added a hike and a ride over the hills. He found the palace ready and waiting for their occupancy. On the evening of October 21, while at the Summer Palace, he received the news of the death of Imperial Noble Consort Duankang. She was a widow of the Guangxu Emperor and an aunt to Tang Shixia.

November 2, 1924

On Sunday, November 2, shortly after dawn, Puyi called a meeting with his most trusted advisors. This included Jung (Wanrong's father) and Cheng Hsiao-hsu.

Cheng was a loyalist who turned down military positions with the Republic. Instead, he preferred to serve the emperor in balancing the budget of the Nei Wu Fu. Cheng had reduced the expenditures by thousands of dollars per month. Puyi wanted Cheng to replace the less trustworthy Shao Ying, but he could only negotiate for the two to work side-by-side. Cheng penned in calligraphy to earn money and was a follower of Confucianism. In 1912, when the emperor was abdicated, Cheng wrote a poem telling of the anarchy to come.

In the meeting, reasons were given for the belief that Feng was planning a coup against the emperor. It might be the same as the plan executed against the president. They discussed taking Puyi to Legislation Quarter for his safety. However, all exits were closely watched. Even at the Gate of Spiritual Valour, the imperial guard had retreated inside to avoid conflict with the military troops. Cheng continued to work out a plan to rescue the emperor. Puyi would need a disguise.

The meeting with his trusted advisors was complete. Puyi gave each advisor an errand. Puyi gave Sir Johnston a bundle of essential documents and a parcel of valuable items. Sir Johnston placed them in a safety deposit box at the Hong Kong and Shanghai Bank (HSBC) in Beijing. The critical documents included the birth certificate of Jin Youzhi, Wenxiu's son. Puyi knew the manners of an English gentleman would prevent him from thumbing through the pages.

Cheng Hsiao-hsu was the last one to leave. Puyi gave Cheng money to pay the servants who cared for Wenxiu's son. To ensure his care, the servants received advanced payment of five years. However, Puyi knew, at some point, the advance payment would run out. He might not find a way to continue paying the hired servants.

Later that same day, Sir Johnston returned from his errand, offered his condolences, and paid his respect to Duankang. The ceremonies that took place were less grand than under normal circumstances. Puyi opened a cabinet and brought out a small basket of jeweled rings. "They were all Duankang's rings," Puyi explained. With a sad facial expression, he added, "They would be stolen if they had been left in her palace. Choose the one you like best and keep it in memory of her." Sir Johnston selected an exquisite green jade ring.

November 3, 1924

On Monday, November 3, many of the servants were moved to safety in the uncertainty of the political situation. These servants included Wenxiu's lady-in-waiting and personal servants of the imperial household. The few that remained wore white in mourning the death of Duankang. They walked at a brisk deliberate pace, carrying out the funeral and ceremonial activities. This gave the Forbidden City a ghostly and forlorn appearance.

November 5, 1924

On November 5, 1924, at breakfast time, the telephones were finally working, but the emperor's own telephone line was cut. The troops had seized and closed the Gate of Spiritual Valour. No one was allowed in or out. Feng revised the "Articles of Favorable Treatment" and, on the same day, exiled Puyi and, with him, the imperial household, including his wife, brother, and sister-in-law. They were given only three hours to permanently leave their home, the Forbidden City. An eviction is never enforced with such little warning. Usually, a tenant is given weeks to pack.

The courtyard was already unusually quiet. Now it was deathly quiet. Puyi took notice of the silence and stillness in the courtyard. "Where are my servants?" Puyi asked the soldier of the National Army.

"There are no servants," answered the soldier. In Asian culture, this means the servants were killed. The servants are no more. The eunuch system was abolished. Only Shao Ying remained. Puyi had fifty servants. This included the Eunuchs of the Presence, his own personal servants, and trusted messengers. The servants were like family to Puyi. News of their deaths was devastating. Puyi explored abolishing the eunuch system, but not like this.

[Youlin interjected with the correction, "Some of the servants survived."]

The soldier asked, "Where are your children?"

"I have no children," Puyi answered. Puyi trained his wives to back up anything he said. Puyi did not want the deaths of any more servants on his conscience, especially those who cared for his son.

Although Wenxiu backed up Puyi, she stirred at his response. He had no children with Wanrong but a son with her. She wondered, "Didn't that mean anything to Puyi?" At the same time, she was aware of their danger. Her attendant avoided death because she was safely outside the Forbidden City.

The revision of the articles allowed them to choose their new residence. The Summer Palace was their choice. However, in the end, there was no option. The Summer Palace, ready and waiting, remained vacant and soon had charged admission. Puyi, Wanrong, Wenxiu, Pujie, and Tang Shixia were sent to an unexpected location in Beijing.

Prince Chun's Northern Mansion

Puyi sat with his father, Prince Chun, and his eunuch, Shao Ying, in the South Hall of the Northern Mansion, trying to figure out what to do. The residence is near the Shichahai neighborhood in central Beijing and Puyi's birthplace. Prince Chun was pacing the floor, occasionally stopping, starting to speak, and then back to pacing. Puyi was concerned, but not as much for himself as for the two High Consorts who vowed death over leaving the Forbidden City. There was no avenue for information. His messengers were gone.

Cheng Hsiao-hsu was the first to involve the Japanese to help Puyi escape his exile. Cheng's plan was vetoed by Puyi's father, Prince Chun. After this Prince Chun would not allow foreigners in or out. However Cheng asked the Japanese to be Puyi's protector. Japanese cavalry agreed to patrol the area. Cheng also maintained a friendship with Hsu Shih-ch'ang, the former president of China.

Restrictions were relaxed and Sir Johnston, who was a foreigner, was finally allowed to re-enter the Northern Mansion. Sir Johnston arrived in the evening. Sir Johnston found everyone together in a large room. He found the situation confusing. He gave them the first news of the outside. Wanrong's father Jung Yuan had entered the hospital with nervous disorders. Sir Johnston acted as another liaison between Puyi and Japan.

Any news of the outside was treasured. Puyi settled for the information available. Pao Hsi looked after the two High Consorts and took them into his home. Puyi was not informed about his son's welfare. The circumstances were too restrictive.

Not long after Puyi was evicted from the Forbidden City, Zhang Zuolin led people into the capital and drove out Feng Yuxiang. Puyi was invited to return to the Forbidden City. Puyi had high hopes for Zhang Zuolin, but he did not dare rely on him completely. Instead, he inclined an ear to his advisors. His advisors pointed him to other paths. Puyi was informed that Zhang Zuolin may not succeed in achieving his goals.

In 1925 Puyi disguised himself as a businessman and went to the Japanese Legation. He was there for a couple of months. Then, after his twentieth birthday, he prepared to go to Tianjin. On February 23, 1925, at 7:00 p.m., he left the Japanese minister and his wife and took a train to Tianjin. His wives were to follow. At each stop, more and more Japanese police and special agents dressed in black boarded the train until the train was full of them. Later Wanrong and Wenxiu were escorted by the Japanese to Tianjin. They were exiled to Tianjin on the coast of the Yellow Sea to the southeast of Beijing. These were cramped quarters compared to what they were used to. Initially, it was three rooms, and then a whole building was cleared out for them.

They stayed at the Chang Garden for five years, rent-free. This was a three-acre lot with a large house. A former Qing general owned it. It was not entirely horrible. There were opportunities for golf, horseback riding, and dancing. Puyi continued his financial support to the servants in Beijing who cared for his son. Puyi's brothers and sisters visited them in Tianjin. Puyi was able to form a bond with his younger half-brother Puren in the absence of seeing his son.

In 1924 this area was conceded to Japan by China. Puyi and Wanrong became commoners. Wenxiu did not perceive a change in her status. From her perspective, she was already a commoner. Wenxiu assumed she was now on equal footing with Puyi.

There were many errors in Wenxiu's perspective. Puyi and Wanrong were noble-born. However, Wenxiu was also a princess under the yellow banner and, as such, was noble born. This status they were born with, no one could take that from them. Puyi was raised to believe it was his place to sit on the dragon throne. The status of the commoner was not to be accepted readily.

Now, more than ever, it was important for Puyi to feel in charge of political matters. He wanted to claw his way back. Cheng Hsiao-hsu came back into Puyi's service. He both praised and criticized ideas and offered original thoughts of his own. He showed no bias or leanings towards any group. He was a perfect political advisor. One time, Puyi voiced his hopes fully to Wenxiu: "It seems that Japan is not bad for the Qing Dynasty." Wenxiu's intuition told her this was wrong. She tried to persuade Puyi not to trust Japan. But Puyi did not listen. Government matters were for the men. Wenxiu felt disregarded.

The battles between China and Japan were as never-ending as the tensions between Wanrong and Wenxiu. They were no longer living in separate buildings. They shared the same house, with Wenxiu's bedroom downstairs and Wanrong's upstairs. Jealously arose between Wanrong and Wenxiu. Wanrong mocked Wenxiu. The two wives were in constant conflict. Eventually, each wife was given an allowance. At first, Wanrong was given $1,000 per month, and Wenxiu was given $800. This was mad money, not for necessity. The free rent did not prevent them from ending in financial difficulties. Puyi reduced their allowances. Wanrong received $300, and Wenxiu received $200 per month.

Puyi's decision and rationale for these amounts was a fundamental change from the wedding day. In preparation for the wedding back in 1922, he wanted them to both receive the same betrothal presents. He wanted them to share the same wedding day. He wanted them to receive the same wedding night and treatment. He wanted them to walk side-by-side during processions. Now he gave Wanrong, as empress, a higher allowance. At the same time, he was no longer an emperor and couldn't justify having a secondary consort. This was a more significant source of the conflict.

August 1, 1927

On August 1, 1927, Communist leader Mao Zedong founded the People's Liberation Army. In 1928 Chiang Kai-shek, leader of the Republic of China, offered to re-negotiate the Articles and allow the former emperor and his court to return to the Forbidden City. Puyi refused the offer. He had other plans. The Japanese cultivated a strong tie with Manchuria for many years, and now Puyi was the leader of the Manchu clan. At this time, Tang Shixia did not continue with them to Japan and parted with Pujie. She distrusted the Japanese.

In 1929, they moved to a palace called the Quiet Garden Villa or Garden of Serenity and stayed there for two years. Puyi stated, "They called it the Garden of Serenity. It was anything but." Ceremony invitations were for the Emperor and Empress and excluded Wenxiu. There was no place for her. Puyi hated this because he could see that Wenxiu was not well. They regretfully left her alone.

Wenxiu saw this as Puyi willfully abandoning her. Wenxiu writes in her diary, "The doe trapped in the garden is like a person locked in a prison who, unless there is a general pardon, will find no freedom," *Forgotten Lives*. She was speaking of herself as the doe. The garden was the palace. Wenxiu spent her remaining years as Consort in Tianjin.

Wenxiu wrote in her diary (paraphrased),
"For my company at night,
I watch the candle flame's light.
When the candle has burned down, and the wick is too tall
And the light dances brightly against the wall.
I use scissors to cut the wick.
I feel like I am the wick."

I'm not sure what the reason was. Maybe it was because she felt like the candle's wick. Perhaps it was because her mother died, and she could not find comfort. Or maybe it was the quip she made to Wanrong about infertility years earlier, telling her to stab her belly. Abandonment from Puyi essentially made her reproductive organs feel useless. Maybe her mother's death was more abandonment. Or perhaps it was a little of all of these. Whatever the reason, when Wenxiu was 20, she attempted suicide by stabbing herself in the abdomen with a large pair of scissors.

Puyi and Wanrong were celebrating a Chinese festival in Tianjin. A eunuch found Wenxiu and ran to tell Puyi. He saw this as a cry for attention. He didn't know how to handle it. He just wanted her to stop. At first, he beat her. Then, for Wenxiu's companionship, Puyi had Wenxiu's younger sister Wenshan join her in Tianjin after their mother died.

Wenshan coached Wenxiu to demand equal rights in marriage. She encouraged her to divorce Puyi. On August 25, 1931, Wenxiu agreed to file for divorce. Wenxiu stabbed herself again in front of Puyi, this time in the neck. She was rushed to the hospital with her sister. After the hospital stay, they checked into the Tianjin National Hotel. They never returned to Puyi.

Wenshan took silver and divided it into three piles to pay the three attorneys she hired. She arranged for the attorneys to stay at the Tianjin National Hotel. The attorneys negotiated on Wenxiu's behalf. Wenxiu's letter to the attorneys stated the main reason for her divorce from Puyi: "For nine years, I have not been fortunate enough. I was lonely and sorrowful. I was abused, and [it was] unbearable. I now request to live away." Nine means an eternity in Chinese. "No luck" might mean the relationship wasn't consummated.

Puyi was extremely angry when he saw this letter because he had no way to explain their son. He immediately sent people to the National Hotel and tried to arrest Wenxiu for interrogation. He just wanted to reason with her. But Wenshan anticipated his reaction and left the hotel with Wenxiu. All they found were Wenxiu's three attorneys. Puyi didn't trust Wenxiu's attorneys to confide in them. They didn't seem to understand the complications this created.

Of course, Puyi thought of Wenxiu as his wife. When they were evicted from the Forbidden City, he argued for her safety from the National Army by stating that she was equally his wife. The original edict only allowed Wanrong to leave the Forbidden City as his wife. Wenxiu's safety was not considered in the eviction. He didn't find a way to tell her; he had loved her best.

Wenshan took over the divorce legalities. She hired the attorneys. She prevented Wenxiu's testimony because she determined Wenxiu was physiologically sick. The divorce procedure regarded Wenxiu as unable to handle her affairs. The attorneys never asked if Wenxiu had any children when they completed the court documents because they assumed they knew the answer. As a result, Wenxiu's son Jin Youzhi was omitted from the divorce paperwork completed by the attorneys. The newspapers published the reason for Wenxiu and Puyi's divorce as, "After nine years of marriage, there was no husband and wife life, and Wenxiu was bullied."

September 13, 1931

Puyi had to let Wenxiu go. He loved her too much to force her to stay. An agreement was reached on September 13, 1931. Originally Puyi wrote that Wenxiu would live out her days in the home he purchased for her family. Unfortunately, the condition was erased because Wenxiu's family had already sold the house. Weniu's attorneys asked for 500,000 Yuan in compensation. This was negotiated down. Puyi paid Wenxiu 50,000 Yuan as lifetime alimony.

October 22, 1931

Yufen, a friend of Wenshan, took some of the money through fraud. The doctor's bill, the stay at the Tianjin National Hotel, and attorney fees were deducted from the total she received. Puyi made sure of it. From then on, Puyi's finances were closely watched. The divorce was formally signed on October 22, 1931.

Wenshan knew Wenxiu was mourning the death of their mother. Wenxiu had not visited her mother before she died and never had the opportunity to inform her of her pregnancy. She was taken away to the Forbidden City when she was only a child of twelve. Wanrong received more visits from her stepmother than she did from her mother. So many things happened, and the moments to share those events with her mother were forever lost.

In the realization of her mortality, Wenxiu yearned to see her son. Her yearning for a child was the desire to see her son. Unfortunately, her younger sister misunderstood this yearning. Wenshan assumed she would be the first to know if her sister was pregnant. However, at the time of the pregnancy, Wenshan was only a child. It would not have been wise to take her into confidence.

After the divorce was finalized, Wenxiu returned to Beijing as the contract required. She rented a house, and Wenshan lived with her. She took employment as a teacher in a primary and middle school, specializing in teaching Chinese literature and pictures. She was recommended for the teaching position, most likely by Puyi. Their son Jin Youzhi was primary school age and living in Beijing. Puyi must have anticipated that Jin

Youzhi would be in the school. However, if Wenxiu wanted to find her son, she needed to look elsewhere.

China 2016 - 2018

In August 2016, President Xi Jinping announced in a speech a request to hold the banner of Chinese unity high. This effort was called Sinicization. Part of China's Sinicization push was to remove mosque domes. This reconstruction began in 2018. Thousands of mosques now have Buddhist tile roofs and are adorned with Buddhist symbols. In some places, the scaffolding remains around the building, announcing it is too unsafe for worship. The intent is to reduce the influence of foreign religions and make Muslims more like China's Han ethnic majority. The Republic added Buddhist adornments even though the political government workers are required to be atheists. The communist party regards atheism as more sensible. Buddhists are barely tolerated, not appreciated.

The Republic eradicated Jews from China. The rationale was that Jews have a foreign religion influence. They put God first before China's leader. Jews pray in Hebrew. The Hebrew language is no longer tolerated in China. The Chinese believe speaking Hebrew allows Jews an opportunity to plan subversive activities.

[Hephzibah gasped, "The Jews are already eradicated. I failed."]

Worshipers in China sign an agreement to put Xi Yinping above God. They read Xi Jinping's words side by side with their religious doctrine. Prayer is no longer allowed in China. Penalties for not complying include long-term imprisonment and even execution. You don't need to be found guilty to receive imprisonment. You only need to be identified as someone likely to offend. They explained, "It is better to re-educate someone before they offend. This is a better program." However, there are no retirement benefits after release from imprisonment, regardless of whether or not there was a conviction.

February 1, 2018

On February 1, 2018, President Xi Jinping passed an extensive set of religious laws to limit the influence of Christianity on Chinese society. The Republic of China banned online Bible sales. Christmas celebrations were banned. The Republic sent anyone publishing Children's Bibles to prison. The Republic offered monetary rewards to citizens who informed on offenders. Authorities pressured landlords to evict churches from rented spaces. The Republic installed padlocks on the doors and posted police officers outside.

Anticipating closures, some churches divided their congregations into small groups and met in homes. These are the groups that came to be known as house Christians. Larger technologically advanced churches moved to online services. Other churches chose to wait until the police closed their doors. Police invited pastors to tea as an opportunity to reemphasize their threats. Now there are penalties for meeting in small groups and penalties for downloading religious podcasts. The Chinese believe they need to be monitored.

[In 2019, Youlin explained to Hephzibah, "We need to make sure they aren't planning subversive activities."

"Subversive?" Hephzibah asked. She wasn't sure about the word's meaning or how he used it.

"Plotting against the government," Youlin explained.

"They are just worshipping," Hephzibah argued. She paused to think and added, "Most Jews don't know conversational Hebrew. They don't plan subversive actions. Ancient Hebrew is the language of their prayers. The prayers are always the same. Their prayers may be pre-approved."

"They are not allowed to pray at all in China, regardless of the language," Youlin's friend informed her. This was not the answer Hephzibah wanted to hear.]

While Youlin was in the United States, the political situation in China was changing rapidly. In response to the economic depression in Asia, Xi Jinping proposed a plan for economic revival. Xi Jinping hoped to resurrect the Silk Road. The approval of his idea led to the removal of presidential term limits in China. This change enables Xi Jinping to rule indefinitely. This change was not only done without the approval of the Chinese citizens. It was done without even informing them. China became a republic with no term limits.

The archeological evidence fails to support the idea of thriving trade along the Silk Road. Each of the sites reported the same lack of evidence. There was not enough trade to improve the economy. Instead, there was an opportunity to share ideas and technology that benefitted both parties. This exposure to new technology was the main value of the Silk Road.

There was one other rationale that led to the decision. Puyi died fatherless. Based on this, the emperor's title should extend to Xi Jinping. But what if that statement is proven to be false? Youlin's work as an engineer requires credibility and trust. He had every aspect of proof for the line of succession. Yet he was doubted. This situation was Youlin's dilemma.

Hephzibah

Hephzibah was hesitantly curious about the books Darius mentioned. She contacted the local synagogue and asked to come in. The Rabbi welcomed her there and into their library, where they had a Torah study. There is a vast collection of books; history, cookbooks, and children's books, but not the one Darius mentioned.

Later she researched the name Hephzibah in the Jewish Encyclopedia. There she finally found the story Darius referred to, The Apocalypse of Zerubbabel. Only this Hephzibah isn't the delight she hoped to be. This Hephzibah was a woman with military skills who destroyed a leader or two and maybe helped to kill a third. Instead of a delight, she appeared to be a dreaded assassin. This revelation was a sinking disappointment, leaving a pit in her stomach. There was no translation in English, only a summary.

She didn't want to read the book. She'd rather live her own life instead of the life of a character in a book. If she tried to live the life of someone in a book, she would miss out on too many things in real life.

The Hephzibah in the Apocalypse of Zerubbabel has a baby, so the character must become pregnant. A man she dated off and on for ten years called and wanted to get together with Hephzibah. He confessed, "For some reason, I want to get you pregnant." She turned him down. As she hung up, she realized she wasn't working to fulfill Zerubbabel's dream. Instead, she was actively crushing Zerubbabel's dreams.

Hephzibah attended a Hanukkah celebration. At the festival, she was consulted on engineering designs. One design was technology that was proven not to work. Hephzibah didn't dash their hope or excitement. She could see what the problem was. She had enough physics, advanced math, mechanical engineering and control programming experience to suggest an easy fix. She corrected the math errors to make the designs work and offered a control design solution to provide the necessary response time. Her corrections were accepted, and the financial donors felt a seal of approval from a physicist and engineer.

In addition, another engineering design of Hephzibah's received $100,000 in donations to the synagogue for labor, supplies, and materials. She tested this design while working on a Master of Science degree in physics, with the help of a doctorate in Mechanical Engineering. Some called this the rod of Aaron. But what stick can strike a rock and have water gush out? It was never the stick dong the miracle. It was always God.

At the Hanukkah dinner, Hephzibah learned the miracle of the olive oil lasting eight days instead of one day. The oil is celebrated instead of the military victory because this miracle came from God. The Jews do not want to honor the violence of the Maccabees. The Maccabees defeated their enemies with the sword. The Rabbis determined this violence was just as bad as the violence they conquered.

If Darius is right, and she is the Hephzibah in Zerubbabel's dream, she would be risking her life for people who believe the pen is mightier than the sword.

Hephzibah and Youlin

Hephzibah was working in a lab testing thermal designs. Heated wind tunnels were part of her graduate research in Mechanical Engineering. This role used those skills. Ralph, her supervisor, walked in and approached her aisle. He was flanked on his right by a man, over six feet tall, with straight black hair. He had skin the color of burnt butter, evenly spaced white teeth, and a huge smile. Ralph introduced, "You are going to be working on the project his group is funding."

Jin Youlin extended his hand. Hephzibah accepted the handshake. His hand was damp with sweat, and he was nervous. Hephzibah put away the test unit she had finished assembling and moved on to another assembly. She looked over at Jin Youlin and smiled. He smiled back. Ralph completed his introductions, including Mike, the lead thermal technician. Ralph explained the project and then left the lab with Jin Youlin.

Mike was a Cantonese man who worked in the lab for five years. He worked on the same aisle in the lab with Hephzibah. He was a short man, five feet tall, broad body, a round face, dark brown freckled skin, and short, layered, straight black hair. He wore black-rimmed glasses.

Jin Youlin scheduled a meeting with Mike, Jake (the Head of the Lab), and Hephzibah. He sent out an email to the participants. Hephzibah was ready to be of total assistance. To complete the certification, he needed measurements and to design a tool to complete the task.

Mike told Jake, "There wasn't much we could do to address Youlin's concern." The supplies they had on hand were designated to other projects. Each plate was a specified weight.

"Well, I'm sorry I came then," Jake laughed. Mike laughed too. Hephzibah had a sinking feeling. This wasn't the way to respond to an engineer's request. Instead, they should be showing respect.

Youlin came into the lab. Mike brushed him off. Jake did too. Jake stood up out of his chair and left the lab. Youlin went to the end of the aisle to grab some tools. Anger and frustration replaced his usual calm look. Hephzibah went over to help him. "I have an hour," he said. He had cleared his busy schedule for the one-hour meeting. Now he was working on etching out a plate to use for testing.

Hephzibah leaned over towards him and said quietly, "I have an hour too. Let me help."

Youlin leaned over and whispered in her ear, "Go back to work." The word "work" was held out extra long. Rather than argue, Hephzibah returned to her workstation. Youlin thought she was flirting with him. She was only trying to show respect to him as a design engineer. It hadn't occurred to her that he would interpret it as flirting.

As Youlin left the lab, Mike commented, "He left here in a better mood than I expected him to." He looked at Hephzibah and asked, "Did you say something to him?" Hephzibah shook her head no. Mike explained, "He's Chinese ... royal class." Mike jumped down off his bar stool. "I'm so over it."

Hephzibah wasn't sure what Mike meant. "Over it?" she asked. She didn't follow what he was saying at all. It seemed too important to dismiss.

"Communism is here to stay," Mike said definitely, briefly turning back to look at Hephzibah, "The last thing I want to see." He spoke the last words of the sentence slowly, in a deep voice, and with emphasis, "Is him breed." His face was in disgust. Mike returned to his thermal test.

Door A or B?

Ralph, Hephzibah's work supervisor, received an anonymous caller who claimed she was romantically interested in him. Ralph and Jake entered the lab together. Ralph asked, "Between the two of us, who would you rather date?"

Jake nodded, "You can date anyone here that you want."

"I'd rather take door #C," Hephzibah responded, thinking about an old game show on television. "Between the two of you, I'd rather date George." George was a short, balding Jewish man who performed thermal and mechanical tests in the lab.

Ralph said, "That's the last time I believe them." Ralph and Jake left the lab.

Genealogy

Mike mentioned that he was planning a trip to Italy. His son was accepted to play the drums on tour. Mike was excited to watch his son play in Italy. He boasted, "I love to sit in the bleachers at the high school with a beaming smile and cheer him on, even if I am the only parent there." He qualified for a sabbatical and the trip to Italy was his choice.

Hephzibah mentioned that she was planning a trip to London. "I have several ancestors who were mayor of London," she explained. She assumed it was okay to mention them. Mike prodded with more questions, and Hephzibah finally admitted that she had the full Plantagenet line. "The kings who made England while living in a trailer and eating peanut butter sandwiches," she joked.

Jin Youlin was one aisle over working on the project. Hephzibah hadn't seen him. He had overheard the conversation. Jin Youlin came around the corner. He said, "I have the Qing line."

Hephzibah exclaimed, "Oh, I know that line." She looked at Jin Youlin and beamed.

"How do you know that line?" Jin Youlin asked curiously. He seemed delighted.

"We thought we had it," Hephzibah explained. "We have the youngest son of four children. The father died, and the mother remarried a Qing. But it turned out all of her children were with her first husband. The Qing was just a stepdad."

Mike rolled his eyes. He saw no possibility a Qing would be a stepdad to one of her ancestors. He also thought Jin Youlin was bragging. Youlin was tall. However, Mike could name other Chinese men who were tall. He remained quiet at the time.

"Do you have Hun?" Jin Youlin asked.

"Yes," Hephzibah admitted. "And you do too. We are both descendants of Attila the Hun." Jin Youlin smiled and disappeared onto another aisle in the lab to finish his test setup. He had the ability to appear and then vanish. The tall shelves of supplies blocked the view of the neighboring technicians and engineers.

However, not long after, Ralph came to a meeting with a new rumor. He said, "I was told you are wrong about your genealogy."

Youlin approached Hephzibah, "Let me help." He asked to do some research to help Hephzibah in her situation.

Hephzibah appreciated his offer to help. The Washington State Attorney General's Office had paid a private investigator. His name was Reuben Campos, P.I. Youlin ordered the results of the investigation. The P.I.'s investigation cleared Hephzibah of wrongdoing. The Washington Attorney General's Office had kept the result of the investigation hidden. They continued when they were required to stop.

Hephzibah gave Youlin the name of her great, great grandfather to start the search. He paid for a genealogical study to affirm her ancestry. He found the genealogy of her great, great grandfather well researched and documented.

Youlin discovered she also had the Kings of Armenia. This line she didn't know about. This included the kings who were exiled by their brother, a Chinese Emperor during the Han Dynasty. The ruler of Turkey gave the exiled brothers the region of Armenia to rule. Hephzibah and Youlin had another common ancestor. Hephzibah hoped the genealogy study would help disprove what Ralph was told and clear her of allegations of dishonesty.

When they had a chance to talk, Ralph corrected, "Actually, it was the Oregon Attorney General's Office who talked to us." At first, Hephzibah was relieved that the Oregon Attorney General's Office was involved. In 2012 someone gave the attorney general false information in an anonymous file. The office caught the mistake and went after the group that gave them the incorrect information.

This time two women attorneys at the Oregon Attorney General's Office misunderstood. They thought "again" meant Hephzibah was a problem before. The attorneys didn't check the accuracy of the claims. The anonymous caller said, "The information was already verified." The Oregon Attorney General's Office assembled a file that regarded Hephzibah as a repeat offender.

There was no place to submit the paid genealogy study Youlin had done or the result of the P.I.'s investigation. The Oregon Attorney General's office misinformed Ralph that Hephzibah was found incompetent. They didn't catch the mistake.

Later the two attorneys with the Oregon Attorney General's Office who assembled the file were fired. After they were fired, their file continued to circulate. When illegitimate files are put into the database, there is no procedure to delete them. The file remains in the database like a computer virus waiting to strike its next unsuspecting victim.

A man, acting on instructions in the illegitimate file, told Hephzibah's employer that she believed she descended from royalty and that she thought Mike did too. Why Mike? They must have meant Youlin. Somewhere in the relay of messages, the names needed to be clarified. Why did the illegitimate file name Mike?

"Mike doesn't want to rule China," the man said.

"I don't want Mike to rule China either," Hephzibah countered. "For one thing, Mike is Cantonese."

"He is from the wrong part of Asia," an Asian coworker clarified.

Hephzibah had no bias against the Cantonese. However, it showed how badly the information was confused.

Later Hephzibah was walking down the hallway back to the lab, very frustrated with the events. "Why does this keep happening? Why do I not have the opportunity to confront the accuser? Or present evidence on my behalf?" she complained silently to herself. "Who continues to do this?" She was angry enough to yell but determined to keep quiet. Hephzibah needed quick answers, but the answers were anything but fast.

A couple of women from the office in the hallway stood next to Youlin. Hephzibah was walking in their direction, the lab door only a little further to the left. They were standing on the right side of the hallway and staring at her. Then, they saw something glowing in her hand. They asked Youlin, "Do you see that?"

Youlin saw it too. "Power," he said. He stared at her and laughed. His smile and his greeting, "Hello," was enough to calm her.

Hephzibah freely let Youlin use the rock with seven eyes. It wasn't his fault there was nowhere to submit the professional study or the DNA results to the Oregon Attorney General's office. He had done his best. She trusted he would use it well. Youlin used the rock to make plans for the future. His goals were to bring peace and unity to the Chinese people. He worked together with the seven eyes to decide what was best. Youlin asked the rock, "Why are you called the seven eyes?"

The seven eyes replied, "I don't know. That is not my name."

Youlin asked, "Why are you called a rock?" The seven eyes didn't answer. He just laughed.

Later Youlin arrived in the lab and told Hephzibah he found the book about her. It was the same book Darius had found. Hephzibah had not mentioned it to Youlin. The translation was Mandarin Chinese. Darius had missed one of the languages. The book is in Hebrew, Arabic, German, and Mandarin Chinese, but not English. The Mandarin Chinese translation describes Hephzibah as a woman, as most translations do. Youlin informed her, "I sent a copy of the book to all of my cousins." The cousins are the children of Puyi's half-brothers.

Now all Youlin's cousins would think she is the dreaded assassin in the book. She had a sinking feeling of dismay. Historically, a Hun princess fights for the Qing. The emperor is too valuable to go into battle. He sends his wife instead. So, she wouldn't only be a peace treaty bride but a warrior princess representing the Qing during battle. Her grandmother didn't warn her about this.

"I'll need to buy something for you to wear," Youlin decided.

"I think I should go barefoot," Hephzibah teased Youlin. She looked up at his face with a mischievous grin. She hoped for a laugh or maybe a smile.

He didn't notice her facial expression. "No, no, no," Youlin fiercely said, shaking his head. His face started to turn red, "That is a terrible idea." He walked away. He had taken her seriously.

Jake said, "I thought they were about to have a moment." Hephzibah shrugged her shoulders and went back to work, although she wished for a moment, or maybe a laugh.

Youlin explored the idea of dating Hephzibah. He paid someone to go onto her Facebook account and provide him with a collection of her pictures. He calculated her net financial worth. He asked about her debts and loans. He asked about her college debts. He investigated her assets and the land holdings of her family. He had property appraisals done. He thought she might sell her house to pay off her loans. But she didn't want to part with the assets.

After Youlin studied Hephzibah's photos and used the seven eyes, Mike complained to Hephzibah, "He looks at you like he knows what is under there." Mike looked over at Hephzibah and frowned. "It's indecent."

Youlin came into the lab to obtain measurements of his design. He said he had forgotten to do so. He also needed to bring a pen and paper to write down the measurements. Hephzibah offered to grab hers out of her bag. "It's okay. Let's do this," he picked up the lab camera. "Let's work together."

He was very close to her now at her back as they took pictures of his design. His arms wrapped around her, and he moved a little closer. Without realizing it, she also took an image of his hand. Her small treasure was a picture of his thumb on a micrometer.

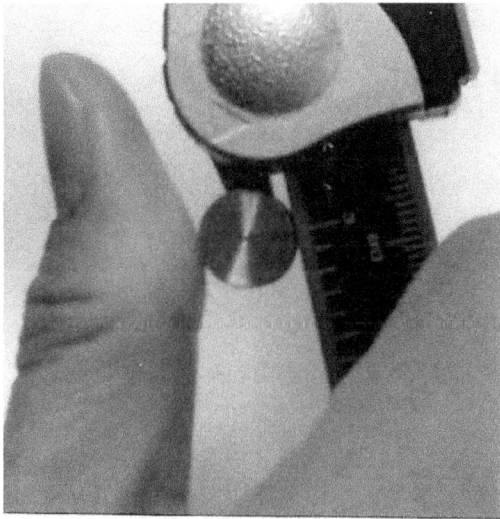

Youlin's thumb

Hephzibah asked Youlin, "Why are your teeth so white?"

He said, "I use baking soda when I brush." He added, "It depends on what type of tea you drink. There are some to stay away from." He thoughtfully paused and then continued, "I've been looking for rooibos tea, and I can't find it."

"Red tea," Hephzibah said. "I used to buy it, and I haven't seen it on the grocery store shelves." She referred to the Celestial Seasonings Madagascar Vanilla Rooibos Tea with a picture of a content lion on the top of the package.

"I'll ship some in from China," Youlin decided. He looked at her and left the lab. He expected that she would take his advice and drink rooibos tea. Instead, she missed the suggestion. Coffee was a habit. As an American she was a beginner at drinking tea.

Hephzibah explained to Youlin that on Passover, she only eats kosher foods. Youlin responded, "I refuse to eat matzah." She decided she could make Jasmine rice, Chicken Pad Thai, Dosa Masala filled with potato curry, or roast duck. These dishes did not contain wheat or leavening. He agreed to these foods. His mother made a big pot of Jasmine rice each day and let him snack on it.

Hephzibah mentioned that she made dragon roll sushi. This is a layer of sticky rice and a layer of seaweed, filled with salmon eggs, seafood, and greens rolled and then topped with avocado slices for the dragon scales, Sriracha mayonnaise, more salmon eggs, and sprinkled with toasted sesame seeds. Youlin paused. He didn't say it, but he didn't like the idea of purchasing salmon eggs. Fish eggs are caviar and expensive.

Youlin liked dosa, a wrap made with rice, black lentils, and fenugreek. "Do you like East Indian food?" Hephzibah asked him. He was confused by the question. Hephzibah explained, "We call it East Indian to distinguish from our misnaming of the Native Americans." At this comment Youlin's college friend laughed.

"Even though India is in the West to me," he solemnly informed her.

Hephzibah was happy to look at things from his perspective. Every day was looking at the world with a new view.

After this, Youlin told his friends he would eat Passover kosher foods. He was joking. However, the cultural differences made him nervous. Hephzibah's religion frightened him the most, even without the mandate of circumcision. "I don't want to attend a service in Hebrew," Youlin complained. "I don't know what I'm saying. I might promise away my first born child." Hephzibah laughed. But Youlin was serious.

Jake asked Youlin, "Can't you just go to the bar and pick up a girl who is drunk?"

Youlin's college friend said, "He can't do something like that."

Hephzibah was nervous about cooking for a man who was Chinese. Thinking hard, she could only name five Asian meals she knew how to cook. Youlin's favorite food was egg rolls.

Hephzibah spent many days and weeks trying to learn how to make egg rolls. At first, they fell apart or stuck to the bottom of the pot. Then they were soggy. She learned to make savory fillings and do an excellent job of sealing them. But she needed to learn how to fry them properly and maintain the oil at the right temperature. So, she tried baking them instead. The baked egg rolls had less fat and calories, but the taste and texture were inferior to the fried ones. The many flopped attempts at egg rolls made her gain weight.

Youlin approached Hephzibah in the lab and asked her, "What does 'gavotte' mean?"

Hephzibah thought of the Carly Simon song, "You're So Vain" She sang the lyrics until she sang the phrase, "You had one eye in the mirror, as you watched yourself gavotte."

Youlin chuckled and said his college friend made the comment about him. Hephzibah watched his gait. The college friend was right. His stride had a gavotte. The next time she saw him walk with a gavotte, she wanted to stab him in the back with a screwdriver. But she quickly hated herself for feeling that way.

Hephzibah was walking up to her building in the early morning. The sidewalk was wet, and earthworms scattered in her path. She paused to rescue a worm before a hurried worker stepped on it. A woman approached her and said, "You aren't ready for him." The woman was discouraging Hephzibah from dating Youlin. She added something that didn't make sense.

Later Hephzibah was soldering test equipment, and Youlin came in to talk with her. He readily found her peering under the microscope with a soldering gun in one hand and lead-free solder in the other. The breeze of the cooling fan was at her neck. "What did they say to you?" he asked Hephzibah.

"I have too many cats," she confessed to Youlin. "I've always trusted Ebony to be clean. He's the one I can count on to use the litter box." She paused and shook her head. "One night, he peed on my computer bag. I heard him and turned on the bedroom light to see who it was. I was surprised to see it was Ebony.

The computer bag was empty, but there was no reason for it. I have three litter boxes he can use. All of them were clean." Hephzibah told Youlin the story to convey her feelings of betrayal. Ebony was her most trusted and clean cat, needlessly peeing in her bedroom. She felt betrayed by his college friend too. She didn't have an opportunity to tell him.

This struggle with Ebony wasn't the answer Youlin was seeking. "What did they say to you exactly?" he pressed, "as you were coming up the walk to the building?"

Hephzibah answered, "She said to me, 'You aren't ready for him. You need to know who is peeing in the corner.'"

Another man working on equipment interjected, "And whether or not it is Ebony." Hephzibah turned to look at him and nodded. At that moment, Youlin darted out of the lab.

Hephzibah turned to see his back. She called out after him as he ran out the door, "I shampoo the carpet." A woman working nearby came over to comfort her. "It just gives him one more reason to reject me," Hephzibah complained miserably.

The woman said compassionately, "I'm not sure he is rejecting you." She consoled Hephzibah by placing a hand on her arm.

Ebony peed on the computer bag because he felt threatened. The same man who took her book on Tao, was on her computer. Hephzibah had another problem to solve.

[Clue #3 Threatened cat. Clue #2 Anonymous file. Clue #1 Missing book.]

Hephzibah hoped Youlin would finish with this exhaustive selection process and move on to a normal courtship. Invite her to dinner, a movie, or a cup of tea. They provided free hot water in the cafeteria. It would take 10 to 15 minutes to have a tea break together. She thought of the selection process between potential candidates 100 years ago. Puyi chose two out of the five. No one hears about the other three and what they went through. Their yearlong, extensive examination only led to disappointment. It must have been uncomfortable. In the end, Hephzibah, too, was not selected. She had gotten her hope up and felt her soul was ripped.

The veterinarian examined Ebony and said, "Your cat is threatened by something. You need to figure out what it is." Hephzibah felt too busy to worry about the cat's feelings. It was enough effort to drive the commute to work, complete her workday, and drive the commute home again. As far as she was concerned, the cat was volunteering to spend more time outside.

Hephzibah was so caught up in this situation with Youlin that she missed something important. Ebony was her cleanest cat. He did have clean litter boxes he could go to. The computer bag was empty. Her laptop was moved to a different place. She wasn't the one who moved the laptop.

Ebony was trying to warn her of a crucial problem. Someone had been on her computer.

Types of Government

Saed, a lab technician from Jordan, described a constitutional monarchy in his home country. Saed was a tall man with broad shoulders, almond skin, dark brown eyes, and thick wavy black hair. He explained the benefits; stability, an opportunity to provide a "vote of confidence," and more satisfaction with the government.

We asked Youlin how he felt about this form of government. We expected him to insist on a monarchy. He surprised us. Youlin shook his head. He said, "The Chinese government should be a republic."

Currently, less than 3,000 Chinese citizens vote. This select group of representatives is employed by the government year-round. They are required to swear allegiance to the President of China. They vow to have no religion. No representative is allowed to regard anyone or anything above the President of China. Decisions and votes are made without consulting the citizens and without informing them of the results and decisions.

Youlin and Hephzibah discussed voting, how often to vote, and the challenges of allowing all Chinese citizens to vote. Youlin hoped for a vote of confidence before the end of term. Hephzibah recognized 1.6 billion votes would need a robust database server to ensure votes are not lost. Ralph was confident his company could design an engineering solution to allow all Chinese citizens to vote. He felt up for the task. Hephzibah's sister, Julia assured Agilent Technologies was prepared with a solution too.

Youlin shook his head and raised the issue that the citizens in the cities would strongly overpower the vote of those in rural areas. It was the science of large numbers. The equation: $A + k = A$ when A is much larger than the value of k. Youlin's background in thermal engineering made the problem more apparent. With this mathematical problem, there was no point in obtaining the vote of all citizens.

Hephzibah explained what they do in the United States for places like Alaska to ensure their vote matters. The US has an electoral college to balance the votes. Youlin suggested using multipliers for geographically large areas with a low population density. Not enough to overpower the cities, but enough to allow them a voice. Under this plan, the Tibetan Buddhists and the Uighur Muslims vote and have an impact. He wanted to keep down the cost of government and avoid an ever-growing number of representatives. Multipliers accomplished this goal.

Problem at the Synagogue

Mr. Cohen, the president at the synagogue said to Hephzibah, "You are in danger."

Later there was a problem at the synagogue. Hephzibah had worked on one of the engineering designs for a couple of years in graduate school. The synagogue used the design and her consults but didn't give her credit for either. The rabbi was concerned about how people would feel knowing the designs came from a woman. Hephzibah hadn't required any payment.

She only asked for membership. But she was denied that too. She tried to voice her objection during a Shavuot celebration. The rabbi looked at her up and down with furry. The power was shut off in the building, and everyone was required to quickly and quietly leave the synagogue in the dark. They were ushered to the front door and told not to speak to each other.

"Well, that was different," they mumbled as they walked out to their cars. The parking lot was dark, but lit with street lights. The open place seemed oddly peaceful after the icy meeting in the stifled room. Now a distance away from the synagogue, they began to wish each other, "Good night!" and, "Have a safe drive home."

Youlin heard about the problem and came to see Hephzibah in the lab. He was concerned about her reaction to the bad news and the rejection. She told him, "I'm going to a book study right now. Regardless of the other issue, I know this is where I need to be." She had found a home at the Orthodox Jewish Chabad. She appreciated Youlin's thoughtfulness. She didn't know how to express her appreciation for his concern and everything he had done for her.

Hephzibah was happy Youlin was planning for the future of China. Youlin also told Hephzibah that she was in danger.

Hephzibah asked Youlin not to lend the seven eyes to anyone else. Youlin wanted to know why. Hephzibah tried to explain with examples of problems that happened in the past. However, despite this, Youlin lent the seven eyes to Jake. Jake used it for erotic entertainment. Hephzibah was outraged and immediately retrieved the seven eyes from Jake. This insulting misuse of something so powerful created unresolvable tension between Hephzibah and Jake. Youlin retained his eye on the east.

Saed could see the Jews did not appreciate Hephzibah. Saed wanted Hephzibah to use her military and engineering design skills to create something for ISIS. He wanted her to help conquer Israel for Allah. He was a supporter of ISIS.

At this time, ISIS was on the border between Israel and Jordan, preparing to invade. Jordan and Israel had collectively built a wall to hold ISIS back from invasion. ISIS remained camped at the edge of the wall. Some Jordanian citizens had become sympathetic towards ISIS. Hephzibah was watching the ISIS movements closely on a government website to receive daily updates.

ISIS was informed Israel had a new weapon. It was one of Hephzibah's engineering designs given to the synagogue. Her friends from her school leaked the information after they helped raise the donations. They told Felicia in Kuwait; and Felicia told her neighbors who were Al Qaeda.

Hephzibah was so proud and appreciative of her friends' belief in her. Her friends donated money and encouraged others to donate; because they knew her as smart.

Saed said to Hephzibah, "We are a holy people. Can't you feel it?" He was tall and bearing over her. He believed the Muslims deserved a holy city such as Jerusalem. "What other city would you have for us?" Hephzibah didn't answer. She just put her head down. He threatened her and pressured her to assist ISIS. She was frightened. Usually, when she is scared, she does not want to see other people hurt. This time she was truly frightened for herself. She felt her life was threatened.

Ralph called them into a meeting. Youlin had bragged to Jake about Hephzibah's weapon design. He felt this was a good engineering accomplishment. He was proud of her. However, Youlin wasn't in the meeting.

Jake told Hephzibah, "I'd think if you were to design a weapon, it would be for the United States." He looked at her solemnly and nodded. For some reason, Jake seemed to be trying to correct her, as if she was confused. Or maybe he thought she was bragging. Hephzibah didn't know where this was coming from.

"It was for Israel," Hephzibah corrected Jake.

"You designed weapons for a foreign country?" Jake exclaimed.

"Are we enemies with Israel now?" Hephzibah asked. "Israel is a small defenseless country. Are we worried Israel might take over the U.S.?" The weapons she assisted with were for defense. Dominion wasn't a goal.

Saed was sitting in the meeting room at the table opposite Jake. Saed said, "Hephzibah might as well design weapons for ISIS." He made the statement matter-of-fact, without emotion. His support for ISIS was clear, even publicly, in the meeting. Now he was trying to get her in trouble at work.

Ralph, their supervisor, told Saed in the meeting that support for ISIS was an unpopular viewpoint. Hephzibah was amazed this was the only reprimand Saed received. ISIS was classified as a terrorist group in the U.S.

In the meeting at work, "I am asking about the green and gold plaid blanket on your bed?" Ralph asked Hephzibah, "Where did you get it?"

Hephzibah thought a man who was a housemate left it behind twelve years ago. "It was Jerry's," she answered. She didn't have a reason to doubt that assumption

"Why do you have it on your bed?" Ralph asked. He was told to ask her the question. "I think I would take it off my bed," Ralph advised.

Why did Ralph ask? How did he know the blanket was on her bed when she never mentioned it? Who was in her bedroom? Who broke into her house? Why did Mr. Cohen and Youlin say that she was in danger?

[All Hephzibah suspected at this point was that her laptop was moved!]

The final question, "Was Ralph implying she stole it?" was an afterthought in comparison to her concerns for her safety and didn't occur to her until long after the meeting.

Jake explained Youlin's rejection to Hephzibah, "Youlin was concerned about the cost of caviar for her sushi dragon rolls. He needed to take into consideration whether he could afford the cost of the ingredients."

Hephzibah explained, "Tabitha works in seafood. The caviar was free. The container was cracked and couldn't be resold. I receive many seafood products this way. The most expensive ingredient is the avocado." She shrugged and said sadly, "I make the dish when I can afford an avocado." Money was tight, so 99 cents was a splurge.

A mechanical test technician said, "Youlin could have gotten caviar for the price of an avocado."

"Actually," Mike said, "Youlin was worried he might gain weight."

Jin Youlin could see and hear Saed's conversation with Hephzibah, even though he was not in the room with her. He went to the lab to speak with her. She was soldering test equipment at a workbench near the lab entrance. The fan was blowing cool air against her neck, calming her nerves. She refused to let Youlin defend her. She stood up to talk with him. She pointed out, "The Qing lived in harmony equally well with both the Jews and the Muslims, even at times when no one else could do so." She did not want him to break his family's 3,000-year streak, not even for her. "I'll find a way to defend myself," she said, shaking her head.

Jin Youlin found it curious that she would think of this political situation and put it above her safety. He was pleased with her and offered to put a Jewish quarter in Beijing. She laughed. Thinking of Jerusalem, she said, "The Jews base their home on a mountain."

He said, "There are plenty of mountains in Beijing." He remembered the hanging monastery. Even as an engineer, he could not understand how the structure was sound.

"What are you, oh great mountain? Before Zerubbabel you shall become a plain; and he shall bring forward the top stone amid shouts of 'Grace, grace to it!'" Zechariah 4:7.

Jin Youlin asked Hephzibah to write a story. There were pictures of his grandmother when she was pregnant, but no one noticed. "What do they want, to see her pregnant and naked?" he grumbled. Hephzibah wasn't sure if she wanted to write about that. The idea of the emperor's wife posing nude was indecent. After returning to calm, he left the lab and went back to his office space.

His idea for a Jewish quarter in Beijing was far from trivial. It isn't because of the land space. There are plenty of mountainsides to build on in Beijing. Inviting Jews back would create a fundamental change in China. It would lean China away from being an atheistic state. Prayer to God would be allowed again.

Youlin complied with Hephzibah's request to remain neutral.

Ralph interpreted Youlin's reaction to Saed's threats was indifference. He assumed this indifference was confirmation Youlin did not care for Hephzibah. Ralph did not know Hephzibah had asked Youlin to stand down. Ralph could not understand why she did this. The situation was precarious at this point.

Saed threatened Hephzibah again. He saw her running towards him. Then he quickly realized she hadn't moved. Then she stepped forward, and it appeared at first as if she remained still. "How can you fight someone like this?" he asked. "I can't tell whether she is moving or not." Each time Saed looked at Hephzibah, he would see a face like an angry white bulldog at her shoulder.

Shortly after this, ISIS withdrew from the Israeli border. Everything they did up to this point was to prepare for the invasion of Israel. Hephzibah's design caused them to turn back. Hephzibah took pride in the accomplishment. This was enough. She did not need to defeat them. She achieved what she intended.

Hephzibah

A Chinese woman working in the lab mentioned that there are 100 million starving people in China. China is a Communist country where everyone is regarded as equal. Some don't have healthcare, while others receive premium treatment. There was a missed opportunity for reform.

Mike thought all countries except for the United States had a problem with starvation. He didn't see China's situation as out of the ordinary. Mike assumed Jordan had starvation problems too. He mentioned this to Saed.

Saed said to Hephzibah, "I don't know why he talks to me like that. We have plenty of food and resources. The only thing we don't have is water." He explained, "People drilled for water sideways, not knowing the problems it would cause to the farmland. So now, it is a desert."

Jin Youlin was around the corner in the lab, working on Mechanical testing. He immediately appeared at the end of the aisle. Then, in a regal tone, he offered to Saed, "If you don't have water, China can sell you water." Then he left the lab to return to his office space.

Mike complained, "I hate it when he talks like that as if he speaks for China." He shook his head. With a frown, he gave an irritated huff and then moved off his stool to pace the floor in the aisle. Hephzibah remained silent and quietly continued to work.

Jake went into the lab and sat down. He absent-mindedly complained, "Nothing is going as I expected." He went back to his office.

Later Jake mentioned in a meeting, "We have no way to calculate the velocity of air traveling through a heat sink."

Hephzibah responded, "That isn't true. We can calculate the velocity of air from the temperature differential." She said it would be too long to elaborate in the meeting.

Jake sent Youlin into the lab to ask Hephzibah how to calculate the air velocity. Hephzibah showed him the mathematical derivation proving the thermodynamic relationship. He started to walk away. She motioned for him to come back. She showed him how to take the derivative, calculate entropy, and the resulting terms that can't be solved. Then she showed him under what conditions those unsolvable math terms go to zero. This was the key to solving the math problem, the beauty of the calculation. She didn't mind too much because she felt she was helping his career. She learned how to calculate enthalpy in her Chemical Engineering and Thermodynamics classes.

Mike watched in surprise. "I wouldn't have done that," Mike said. "Now they have no reason to keep you." With the information passed on to Jin Youllin, she no longer had value to the company.

The next day Jake was gone. "Where is Jake? I need to ask him what the priorities are," Mike asked Hephzibah. Jake had already programmed priority numbers into the spreadsheet, so all anyone needed to do was check the spreadsheet. We had a meeting on this. Mike must have known that.

"Where is he? He's a good person," Mike demanded Hephzibah. She didn't know where Jake was. Had he gotten into a car wreck? Mike sent Jake an email message.

Hephzibah was asked to leave without an explanation. Mike walked her to the door without a word.

[Clue #4 Intuitive hunch that Daniel is violating a Protection Order.]

She stopped to talk to security to let them know she would be filing a police report. The situation needed to be documented. The police officer returned her telephone call and said he didn't see anything illegal. In 2012 they were more thorough. But there was nothing else that could be done now that she was terminated from her job.

July 2019 to February 2020

In July, Youlin had a friend from college who argued that the religious population in China was only marginal and not worth appeasing. The argument was convincing. In truth, the total of China is so large that this marginal population is more than the entire population of the United States. Youlin's friend wanted to go to Mardi Gras in New Orleans as long as it wasn't a religious celebration. Youlin wasn't sure if he wanted to go, but his friend was eager to try it. Participation seemed to be a test of loyalty in their relationship. So Youlin booked the airplane tickets and hotel for the event in February.

Youlin's friend went back home to visit family in December 2019. The hometown was Wuhan City. The COVID-19 virus was about to strike in full force. The blackbirds flew into Wuhan City so thick they looked like a woman's black veil covering the sun in mid-day. The birds arrived to devour what the virus had not. It was impossible to go outside and not be covered with flies. The smell in the air was pungent. At first, they were allowed to clean the apartment of a neighbor who was taken to the hospital. Then they were not allowed to enter the apartment to feed or walk their dog. Then the hospitals were full.

Water dripped dirty from the tap as workers hauled buckets up the side of the buildings to clean out the human waste. Tall apartment buildings were once full of people who lived without indoor plumbing. An open sewer system is a building where men stand and pee in the corner. The collage of umbrellas passing below was never because of rain. The removal of shoes after passing below a building was never because of mud. It was something they didn't talk about in China.

Youlin never heard from his friend again. In February, the flights to Louisiana were canceled due to COVID. The hotels were closed down. There were no refunds for Mardi Gras bookings. Puyi warned his father never to have two women, saying one went away and the other went to the hospital. This worst nightmare happened to Youlin.

Youlin's father died. Due to the COVID restrictions, Youlin could not fly home to Beijing. He was an only child. He always kept his VISA in good standing so that he could return home. The funeral of his father was the most important event. He never wanted to miss. Youlin hasn't been the same since the loss. His mother told him, "Your father wanted nothing more than to see you married and having a child before he died."

Youlin regretfully answered, "I know."

Puyi 1931

The hired servants in Beijing who cared for Puyi's son were no longer receiving payment. The Japanese authorities kept a close watch on Puyi's finances. Puyi was in the position he knew would eventually come. He had no method of paying the servants who cared for his son. Jin Youzhi was now eight years old. The training for polite society was no longer a focus. Instead, the focus was on survival. Admitting he was the son of Puyi would mean imprisonment or, worse, death. Youzhi could not attend public schools. He stood out like a sore thumb because of his height. He was so much bigger and taller; he passed for a teenager.

They needed to find work to survive. Youzhi's height helped the family secure jobs. People saw this tall, strong boy and were willing to hire the family. Puyi's son Jin Youzhi was such a hard worker they did not mind having him with them. At the same time, Jin Youzhi felt an obligation toward the servants and did his best to provide for them financially. He saw the servants as family. He viewed the father of the servants as his own father and sought to emulate him. Puyi would be furious if he had known. In many ways, Jin Youzhi was abandoned by his parents, a forgotten casualty of divorce.

Would anyone have taken in Puyi's son? Maybe, but Prince Chun was under house arrest when he housed Puyi. What type of life would they have if they took in Puyi's son? There were less than a handful of people who knew of the child. Puyi was unable to return to Beijing. He was essentially a political prisoner of Japan. Puyi would not have been able to take him in. Puyi's loyal friend Cheng Hsiao-hsu was busy trying to find a way for Puyi to escape his circumstances. Puyi's father, Prince Chun, would panic at another house arrest. Meanwhile, the servants were concerned for Youzhi's safety and didn't know what else to do. They were of the mind to roll with the crisis instead of voicing a complaint.

Puyi stipulated that Wenxiu return to Beijing as part of the divorce edict. Puyi expected Wenxiu to reconnect with their son when she returned to Beijing. Puyi anticipated that the lifetime alimony would go toward both Wenxiu and Jin Youzhi rather than to Wenxiu and Wenshan. The original edict required Wenxiu to live in providence in the house Puyi bought for her family. Puyi expected Wenxiu would provide for Jin Youzhi's care in that house. Wenxiu couldn't return to the house Puyi bought for her family. When her mother died, her stepfather sold it. The media watched Wenxiu's movements. She may have wanted to avoid exposing her son for his safety. Or she may have questioned her sanity, increasingly so with Wenshan's prodding and Jin Youzhi's absence in the schools.

Wenxiu's younger step-brother took out an article in the newspaper reprimanding his sister for not appreciating everything the Qing had done for their family. This led to bad press and poor public opinion of Wenxiu. Wenxiu was constantly followed. Every day in class, she could hear voices outside her classroom of curious parents wanting to see the strange woman who dared to divorce the emperor. She finally quit her job as a teacher. Wenxiu took her last bit of alimony money and bought a house. Her sister moved in with her. Times were difficult. China was at war with

Japan; her father and mother died, and she had a teenage sister to support. She became poor until the end of the Second Sino-Japanese War.

Tokyo now ruled a large part of China. The Japanese authorities installed Puyi as the new Emperor of Manchukuo, a state in Manchuria, and his wife Wanrong as the Empress. Cheng Hsiao-hsu became the prime minister. Wanrong did not trust the Japanese and preferred to stay in Tianjin. But when Puyi was not allowed to return, she joined him in Manchukuo. Although they held the titles of Emperor and Empress, they were Japanese prisoners from 1934 to 1945.

It was not long before Puyi saw this as a mistake. At the first ceremony, there were Japanese prostitutes. One of the prostitutes asked Puyi if he was in trade. She meant the opium trade. Puyi was offended. This was met with hysterical laughter from the Japanese. The once reasonable Wenxiu had protested against trusting the Japanese to the extent of driving Puyi out of her bedroom. It seems she was not so wrong after all.

Jin Youzhi heard Puyi had gone to Japan. He was told Puyi was there voluntarily. Youzhi didn't know Puyi was not allowed to leave Japan. With Puyi in a foreign country, it was clear that Youzhi was in Beijing with his servant family to stay. The situation was uncertain; however, they made the best of it.

April 3, 1937

Pujie, Puyi's brother, formally divorced Tang Shixia. After graduating from the Imperial Japanese Army Academy, Pujie agreed to an arranged marriage. He selected the Japanese noblewoman Hiro Saga from a photograph of possible candidates presented by the Kwantung Army. The April 3, 1937, wedding at the Imperial Army Hall in Tokyo fortified relations between Japan and China. In October 1937, the couple moved to Hsinking, the capital of Manchukuo, where Puyi was emperor. Hiro Saga gave birth to two daughters, Huisheng and Husheng.

The Japanese officially regarded Pujie as the first in line to succeed his brother as the emperor of Manchukuo. However, Pujie was not appointed by Puyi as the heir to the throne of the Qing dynasty. They assumed this was an oversight. Imperial tradition stated that a childless emperor is to choose his heir from a subsequent generation instead of from his own generation. Another error was in the assumption that Puyi had no children.

March 1938

It is interesting to note that Pujie was not informed of Puyi's son in the same way that Wenshan was not informed of Wenxiu's son. Even the closest family members were left out of the information. But they were only children at the time. They weren't old enough to know how to keep secrets.

The only two who knew of Puyi's child were Cheng Hsiao-hsu, the prime minister, and his father, Prince Chun. Chen Hsiao-hsu died on March 28, 1938.

Sir Reginald Johnston, who knew the location of Puyi's essential documents died on March 6, 1938. He hoped to have the biography published in Chinese, but the attempt was unsuccessful. His biography, "Twilight in the Forbidden City" was banned in China. The biography recorded the location of the safe deposit box that held Puyi's documents.

Wanrong's Affair

Puyi discontinued sexual intimacy with Wanrong when Wenxiu left. He felt Wanrong had driven her away. Later Wanrong had an inappropriate relationship with Puyi's personal guard. Wanrong became pregnant. She continued to use opium during the pregnancy and gave birth to a child. Puyi knew the child was not his. He had not been with her, and he discovered she was having an affair before the child's birth. He threw Wanrong's infant into the incinerator. Wanrong collapsed at the death of her child. After this, Wanrong spent all day smoking opium.

Puyi would not have thrown away Wanrong's child unless he had received news his son was doing well. A fatherless man doesn't throw away a baby, regardless of the circumstances. Messengers would come to speak to Puyi alone. They refused to say what transpired. Some suspected a sexual liaison between Puyi and the messenger. But at that time, Puyi would receive information on his son's well-being.

Wenxiu 1945

In 1945 after the end of the Second Sino-Japanese War, Wenxiu joined the newspaper as a proofreader at a friend's recommendation. The president of the newspaper noticed Wenxiu's hard work and believed her to be a never-married virgin. He wanted to find a husband for her. Liu Zhendong was single and in his forties. The president introduced him to Wenxiu.

Wenxiu after her divorce from Puyi

In the summer of 1947, Wenxiu married Major Liu Zhendong in Beijing. He was a soldier of the Kuomintang army when they met and relied on his own ability to become a major. He was a self-made man. They lived in a rented house in Beijing. Liu was now retired from the military and opened a car rental business. Unfortunately, the car business ran into financial trouble and went bankrupt.

November 29, 1948

On November 29, 1948, the People's Liberation Army entered Beijing in the Pingjin Campaign. The campaign lasted until January 31, 1949, and resulted in a Communist victory. After that, the members of the Kuomintang Army were required to register. The major did not want to register. He was apprehensive because of the campaign in Beijing, the civil war that opposed the Communist Party. He did not know what the Communist Party would do to him.

October 1, 1949

The Communists took over China on October 1, 1949, when Mao Zedong founded the People's Republic of China. The communist government may have affected private enterprises, resulting in their poverty. China was transitioning from capitalism to socialism during this period in a five-year plan. Private enterprises were encouraged and continued to grow. However, some sectors, such as transportation, were now state-run. The following may be factors to the bankruptcy:

1. The economy was already poor from war and civil unrest.

2. A change in government would increase uncertainty and reduced spending.

3. The state-run transportation most likely impacted the major's car rental business.

Wenxiu persuaded Liu Zhendong to confess his membership in the army.

Lui confessed and was handed over to the government for supervision and control. In 1951 he regained his freedom and became a cleaner.

Liu and Wenxiu moved to a small house of ten square meters and started a new life running a cleaning service and manufacturing wooden pallets. Wenxiu worked at the cleaning service. Wenxiu now had the task of a eunuch of the lowest grade. She went from the emperor's consort to a commoner with $800/month in mad money to a cleaner removing human waste off the sidewalk.

In August 1953, Wenxiu confessed to Liu Zhendong that she was married to Puyi as his secondary consort. The divorce edict had restricted her from discussing the union.

September 17, 1953

One month later, Wenxiu died from a heart attack in poverty in a small one-room apartment at the age of 43 on September 17, 1953, with Liu holding her hand.

Liu constructed a coffin himself with four wooden boards the working cleaning team had found. Wenxiu was buried deep in the ground under the loess in the Andingmen district of Beijing.

Liu attempted to sue Puyi on behalf of Wenxiu for an unhappy marriage, but he was unsuccessful. Wenxiu had agreed not to ask for anything more.

December 4, 1957

In 1957 when Pujie's oldest daughter Aisin-Gioro Huisheng was nineteen, Pujie arranged for her to marry. Pujie wanted to strengthen the royal line. Huisheng objected. On December 4, 1957, Huisheng disappeared with her classmate and lover, Takemichi Okubo. On the same day, she was shot by Okubo in Mount Amagi, Japan. It was a murder-suicide. From Huisheng's perspective, it would just be murder. Okubo had already purchased the gun. This subtle difference affects the line of succession.

Hephzibah and Youlin

Hephzibah tried to learn Mandarin Chinese. She borrowed books and CDs from the library. She learned how to construct basic sentences. But in the end, all she could say in Chinese was, "I want Youlin." The foreign language study made her too sad to continue. So, she returned the books and CDs.

Hephzibah went home. She felt uneasy and nervous. She didn't know why. The reasons are so many; I listed them in a different book.

Hephzibah drew her finger through the air. The rock with seven eyes pulled a rip in space. White flames shot up four feet. The flames followed her as she walked down the hallway. She hadn't noticed the flames. She could only see that this was a window into another place and time. This was beyond the ones and zeros of digital space. It was something almost tangible. You could practically reach out and touch it. She never imagined this might be a two-way window.

Even though they were thirty miles apart, Youlin could see Hephzibah rise in the morning and undress to take her shower. He could see her curves. He could smell her Calvin Klein euphoria perfume. He could see her when she was ill, which wasn't so pretty. He could see her lying in bed. He would snuggle up next to her. Her presence was so real to him; he could listen to her cat purring. He could hear her alarm every frik'&# morning at five a.m. playing Tchaikovsky's Dance of the Sugar Plum Fairy. But he could turn it completely off if he wanted to and roll back to sleep. Yet, her early rise and his late sleeping was a reminder of their differences.

Hephzibah could see and smell him, knowing he wasn't entirely there. The smell was him or possibly the smell of his bedroom, old gym socks, and something unpleasant like urine. She wasn't sure if she could live with his standard of hygiene. But, on the other hand, she didn't mind his presence. It was comforting.

The smells weren't traveling through digital space. Instead, Youlin could smell Hephzibah's perfume; because, he had bought a bottle for himself. He complained about the expense. The cost was more than he expected. However, he gave in anyway. He reasoned that he could give it as a gift. Unfortunately, he could never bring himself to ask another woman to wear it.

The unpleasant scent in Hephzibah's house came from the raised floorboard in the hallway. Someone lifted the floorboard a crack to let light in through the carpet to the crawl space below. That same person was directly below her now. That was the person she could smell. That is why she felt uneasy and nervous when she returned home. This was the reason she needed Youlin by her side. Hephzibah was caught up in the moment and didn't connect the critical information.

Later she complained to one of Youlin's friends about the smell. All Youlin said was, "Do I need to take a shower?" He was reasonable. She admitted she was not. She swallowed her pride and her complaint. She admitted she was not the right person for him.

Hephzibah voiced her boundaries at Youlin, following her into the bathroom, looking into the trash can near the toilet for used pads, and counting in a whisper while touching his thumb to the fingers of his other hand. "How weird!" she said. "Some things are just private." At the same time, Hephzibah wanted to talk with Youlin in person to tell him to respect her privacy. She could no longer see him or speak to him. But, maybe, he heard her objection before the connection was dropped.

Youlin counted the number of days since Hephzibah's last menstrual cycle. He wondered if Hephzibah was pregnant and expressed his suspicions to Jake at work. This idea met opposition. Their work supervisor, Susie, voiced her disbelief. Susie reasoned that, certainly, Hephzibah was playing a trick or at least being dishonest about being pregnant. Hephzibah hadn't claimed to be pregnant. This was Youlin's idea. Youlin responded to Susie, "You're forgetting. I see her naked." His comment didn't help at all.

Susie assumed this was poor English. So, she reached out to a Chinese-to-English translator. "I can't understand what he means by that," she expressed concern to the language translator.

The translator replied, "He means he sees her with her clothes off, and you've forgotten that." It was plain and simple. There was nothing wrong with Youlin's English.

Youlin suspected that someone had been in Hephzibah's bedroom, going through her belongings, her nightstand by her bed. He wanted to put his words into English. He thumped his hands together, trying to find the right words. His face had a look of determination and alarm. He stopped without finishing his sentence. He went back to his office. This left Hephzibah confused.

2020

Someone intervened and prevented further conversations between Hephzibah and Youlin. COVID restrictions prevented anyone from going to the movie theater without submitting their name and contact information. And the closest movie theater with its doors open was in Scappoose, Oregon. However, it didn't prevent a strange woman from walking straight into Hephzibah's house. "The door was open," the woman lied. The door was closed again. Hephzibah checked. It was only open when the woman forced her way through it.

"The door is never open," Hephzibah replied as she walked from the bathroom down the hallway to the living room. Hephzibah always closes the front door. The strange woman nervously backed up, sat on the sofa, and looked straight at Hephzibah. Her hands were folded in her lap. She had short blonde hair. She was tall and professionally dressed, not a typical vagrant, but with no facemask. No one can even go to the local grocery store without a facemask, and she just walked straight into a stranger's house.

"I want you to stop contacting Youlin," the strange woman demanded. Who was this woman who wanders into a stranger's home in the middle of quarantine and makes demands? "Would you do it for Intel Corporation?" she asked.

"That's an interesting question," Hephzibah thought, "Why Intel?" Hephzibah turned on her. "Does Youlin agree to this?" Hephzibah inquired. "Do you have anything to show this is his request?" Hephzibah asked. The strange woman didn't answer. Instead, she continued to stare at Hephzibah. "I thought so," Hephzibah responded.

Next, the woman started to look intently around the room as if looking for something to use against Hephzibah in court. She studied the small knickknack on the shelves and the pictures on the wall.

Finally, Hephzibah walked over to the front door, opened it, and gestured for her to leave. "Get out," she demanded. "You're not normal." When the woman was finally outside, Hephzibah told her, "You'd better check the breaking and entering laws."

"It's your word against mine," the strange woman responded. "Do you think you can stand up to me in court?" The strange woman expected Hephzibah to shrink at this comment. Hephzibah contemplated and failed to figure out why this woman expected her to feel ashamed. This strange woman thinks the court wouldn't believe her.

[Clue #5 Woman thinks Hephzibah's testimony would not stand up in court.]

The next-door neighbor came outside, witnessed the conversation, and provided backup. The strange woman left. Her car was on the other side of the hedge, so Hephzibah could not read or report her license plate number.

Later, the strange woman came to Hephzibah's work. She said she was told Hephzibah pled guilty to making a false complaint. She was referring to a blank document. Hephzibah had no idea the blank document had anything to do with accusations of a false complaint and no idea it would be interpreted that way. She explained the paper was blank.

"So, you didn't know what you were confessing to?" the woman asked.

"No, I knew what I was confessing to," Hephzibah answered. "They didn't know what I was confessing to." She sent a postcard to her professor who had her promise to stay in contact, and that was the only thing she had done.

The woman thought Hephzibah was not allowed to use her college degree. Hephzibah corrected her. The attorneys who put together the anonymous file were fired.Later the woman was prosecuted.

[Clue #6 Anonymous file claims she pled guilty to filing a false complaint.]

September 2020

A Han Chinese woman named Moonrise became interested in Hephzibah's situation. (Moonrise is not her real name.) Moonrise was a young woman in her twenties, about 4 feet 9 inches tall, whose short bobbed hair bounced with every step.

Youlin called to ensure all was well with Hephzibah because he was worried about her. It was easy to talk with Moonrise. They both spoke Mandarin Chinese. As a result, Moonrise believed Hephzibah about Youlin being a descendant of the imperial family. She wanted to know Youlin's political beliefs. Based on these political beliefs, she polled Chinese citizens and members of the Chinese military on what they would do, given specific conditions. The conditions were:

1. Citizens would vote between at least three candidates who had previously presided over China.

2. The current administration and president could also be on the ballot (increasing the number of candidates to at least four).

3. Every adult Chinese citizen would be allowed to vote.

4. Low population density regions would receive a multiplier.

The idea was very popular with Chinese citizens and the Chinese military. Currently, citizens in the Chinese military services cannot vote—representative votes for them. The representative may not reflect their viewpoint. Sometimes the representative can be made uncomfortable if they hesitate to vote in a certain way. It is easy to be prosecuted for political views. Candidates become eliminated in this way. Representatives may even disappear. Some people in the United States say, "Can't they just vote out Xi Jinping when his term comes up?" Hephzibah reminded them the term limits were removed. There are no term limits for the president of China.

In alarmed response to this poll, Xi Jinping passed the Five Never Agrees on September 3, 2020, and presented these in a speech to the Chinese people during a celebration of the anniversary of the Sino-Japanese war. The Five Never Agrees makes it illegal to decouple communism from the Chinese people. The law would be enforced internationally. Hephzibah was watching the Chinese news closely at this time. She was not surprised when Moonrise approached her that day and said, "I cannot help."

Hephzibah gently responded with, "I understand." Nothing more needed to be said. Hephzibah appreciated what Moonrise had done so far, and she did not want her to suffer repercussions. Moreover, she needed to protect Moonrise.

After the presidential election in the United States, A businesswoman approached Hephzibah in the parking lot in the early morning hours. The woman walked briskly towards Hephzibah, her high heels clacking on the concrete sidewalk. The woman, dressed in a dark gray suit, introduced herself as an advisor to the Joe Biden administration. Hephzibah looked her over, expecting that her suit would be navy blue. The woman's gaze remained focused on Hephzibah's face, and she said, "I flew from Washington D.C. directly to speak with you."

Hephzibah pointed towards the west. Youlin would be a better choice for a conversation. Hephzibah didn't have a chance to say it. The words had formed in her mind but hadn't yet traveled to her tongue. Her next thought was "caution."

The woman insisted rather pointedly, "I came to speak with you." Hephzibah thought this was strange. The advisor wanted to know the terms of the conditions for the Chinese military. Hephzibah explained these to her. This negotiation was intended to be a win-win. It would significantly reduce blood-shed. The presidential advisor told her, "You had no right to do this."

Hephzibah started to explain, "This was agreed upon while Donald Trump was president." But this wasn't about one president or the United States. This was about China. There were more important problems to worry about. "This was before the Five Never Agrees was passed into law in China," Hephzibah continued to explain. The Five Never Agrees can be enforced internationally." This is where her concern was.

"Well, see about that!" the advisor said. She discussed the possibility of requiring the Five Never Agrees to be repealed. Hephzibah hadn't thought of that. Maybe this meeting was helpful after all. With the Five Never Agrees, one important candidate would be missing from the ballot. That problem could be corrected.

Hephzibah explained it was at her previous job that many of these conversations took place. She described her situation there, "A man who favored ISIS threatened me."

The advisor said, "We don't need a man who is for ISIS in the United States." She added with a nod, "This conversation never happened." She looked at Hephzibah in alarm. Hephzibah didn't agree; she just stared at her.

It needed to be clarified whether the Joe Biden administration would honor the terms. Hephzibah made it clear she intended to enforce the Chinese people's conditions and vote. Regardless of the election outcome, their vote would stand. Hephzibah thought of using a cane on those who refused to honor it. Just then, the advisor saw Hephzibah move. But Hephzibah hadn't moved. Hephzibah remained perfectly motionless. She only appeared to move.

The advisor slowly turned and looked toward the group in the smoking section of the parking lot. This was the group she questioned when she first arrived. Then she turned back towards Hephzibah. She said, "When I showed them your picture, they said, 'Oh, you mean the mother of the messiah. She's right over there,'" She asked, "What did they mean by that?"

It was too much to explain. The reference became confused with the Virgin Mary. Trying to explain all this causes people to assume that she thinks she is the character in the book. Then they nod and say they understand. This nod of understanding means, "I think you are crazy." Then she knows they got it wrong. She's had to learn the hard way to let these comments slide.

Hephzibah explained, "It is a misnaming. The reference is to Hephzibah, not the Virgin Mary. The name means his delight in Hebrew. I am a direct descendent of the prophet Isaiah through his daughter Hephzibah."

The advisor looked her over carefully. Then she decided it was time for the flight back to Washington, D.C. The time difference makes the flight quick coming in but long on the way flying back. She did not need to book a ticket for the flight. All she needed to do was return the rental car.

Even though Hephzibah and the presidential advisor were alone, Youlin could hear the conversation. He noticed the subtle parts of the conversation that Hephzibah had missed. Hephzibah was relieved that he already knew and understood. She didn't know how to explain the situation to him. Although she might find his ability annoying, this time, it was advantageous. Youlin was concerned about their compliance with the conditions.

Later Youlin assumed Hephzibah moved away. Now he didn't know where she lived or worked. A supervisor at Hephzibah's work was yelling at her, so close to her face she could see and feel his spit fly. The supervisor took her into a backroom office and started drilling at her. She had been doing the work of two people, filling in for an absent employee while doing her own job, and failing. The expectations were impossible. He accused her of not being able to multi-task. From his perspective, multi-task means doing the most critical tasks and dropping the trivial tasks. His delivery was anything but supportive. He also assumed she was incompetent, as evidenced by her relationship with a so-called "emperor." He referred to Youlin as "the emperor."

Youlin saw that Hephzibah was in trouble. He was so connected to her when she was in distress that he could hear the discussion. He became unglued. He didn't know where she was located. All he knew was that she was being attacked and demoted for believing he was the emperor's grandson. He contacted the main regional office on her behalf. Thankfully the main regional office treated him as if he was royalty. Hephzibah retained her position at her work.

Later Youlin contacted Tom to deliver a message to Hephzibah. Tom went to talk with her.

"Why doesn't he just come by to see me?" Hephzibah asked. She was becoming tired of a third-party delivering messages.

"He expected you would come by to see him," Tom answered.

"I don't know where he lives. I think I know the city," Hephzibah contemplated, "But I have no method to find a rental. I know sometimes he works from home. During the pandemic, he worked 100% from home. I imagine that would have changed now. I don't know his work schedule."

"He doesn't know where you live," Tom answered, "Not even the city."

"How could he not know where I live?" Hephzibah asked. "He had a property appraisal done on my house, so he knows my address."

"He thought you sold it," Tom answered.

"Sold it?" Hephzibah exclaimed.

"He thought you took advantage of the property appraisal," Tom replied. "He was certain he saw someone else living at the house." Hephzibah could only think Youlin had the wrong address.

[Clue #7 Youlin saw someone living in Hephzibah's house.]

"One other thing," Tom said. "You were told by the authorities in London that he tried to get a VISA to join you but couldn't."

"Right," Hephzibah affirmed. "It was nice for him to try," she said softly with a smile. His effort was endearing. It meant he cared about her.

Tom's response hit her with a jolt. "He is trying hard to figure out why they said that," Tom replied. "He didn't file for the VISA." He added, "Your mother told him you were dating someone else."

"That I was dating someone else?" Hephzibah exclaimed. "Why?"

[Clue #8 Dating life prevented. Clue #7 Someone living in her house.]

Puyi 1959 - 1967

In 1959, Puyi was finally able to return to Beijing. Mao Zedong pardoned him after making his confessions. In every way, he retired as an ordinary citizen, noticing his failings as a ruler and husband. From the time he was evicted from the Forbidden City to this juncture, he had no opportunity to see or acknowledge his son. After Prince Chun's death and before Puyi was released from re-education, the laws of royal succession were rewritten. The royal succession was passed from Puyi to his half-brother Pujie. Aisin-Gioro Husheng is the only child of Pujie, who remains alive. She was born in Tokyo, Japan, in 1940. As a result, the Tokyo-born Husheng represents the Chinese monarchy.

First, Puyi worked in the mechanical repair shop of a botanical garden. The government constantly watched him. Then, he married a fifth wife in 1962, a Han Chinese woman named Li Shuxian. Li Shuxian followed him and reported on his activities. But the twice-divorced Puyi could not bear the thought of another divorce.

Later Puyi became a researcher at the Institute of Literature and History under the Chinese People's Political Consultative Conference. This position gave him more freedom to move around. By this time, his son was in his thirties. Jin Youzhi continued to work in hard labor. At this same time, Communist propaganda described the Qing dynasty as spoiled brats. Puyi's son kept a low profile. Jin Youzhi was raised to believe it was not becoming to parade around as the emperor's son. But the propaganda as a spoiled brat while working hard labor must have stung.

Puyi was surprised to learn Wenxiu had never come to visit Jin Youzhi. Puyi had hoped to reconnect with Wenxiu through their son. In Puyi's autobiography, we read he assumed Wenxiu had never remarried. He did not know Wenxiu had died. He expected the news of her marriage and death to be in the newspapers.

Puyi warned Jin Youzhi, "Do not ever marry two women. I loved Wenxiu best, but I could not find a way to tell her. I had two wives. One [second wife] went away, and the other went to the hospital. So I ended up alone." The two wives he was referring to were Wenxiu and Tan Yuling. Puyi kept a photo of Tan Yuling until the day he died.

Jin Youzhi hoped to marry a titled woman. He thought he might have an opportunity to continue the dragon throne like his father. However, when Puyi completed his rehabilitation, he accepted the role of citizen. He truly internalized it. It wasn't an act. He had nothing to pass on to his son. Puyi strictly told Jin Youzhi not to think of himself as better than his cousins. He was to remain humble. Puyi visited his son a few times. Puyi's brothers, nieces, nephews, and cousins came to know Puyi's son, but they didn't blend as a family.

The Cultural Revolution provided a new reason to keep the secret of his birth. Life was made difficult for anyone who identified with the old regimes. Before he died, Puyi had prepaid attorneys on retainer. They took a blood sample of Jin Youzhi's DNA into court and proved Puyi did not die fatherless. The attorneys ensured that Jin Youzhi's identity remained protected. The political environment made this necessary.

Puyi died of cancer on October 16, 1967. After recovering consciousness for the last time, he gathered all his remaining strength and begged his wife Li, "Please, please bury my ashes at the side of my adoptive father together with Yuling and you." Li did not have the finances to carry out the request. However, 28 years later Zhang Shiyi offered to cover the burial expenses. They were buried together in Xi Ling (the Western Tombs).

Hephzibah

Youlin did his best to address Hephzibah's situation. Youlin stepped in to help her when she was treated as incompetent for believing he was the grandson.

Hephzibah realized he had his own battles with convincing others.

Youlin had experience proving genealogy because this hit home. He took those same steps to prove his.

Hephzibah didn't think about it because she believed him so readily.

All Youlin needed to do was lean towards her and say to her in a whisper, "That's me."

Hephzibah apologizes to Youlin, who is doing everything humanly possible to help. All of his efforts are very much appreciated. He tried to express his suspicions in English but couldn't quite form the words. This can be a problem in any language. The areas where he helped her most reflected his personal struggle.

Youlin said, "Your mother." No other words. No explanation. There was no opportunity to have him expand on the comment or explain.

Hephzibah spun the two words over in her head, as if turning them around multiple times would increase their meaning. She knew they were important.

Holidays, weddings, and funerals are an opportunity for families to gather. This occasion was a funeral. A beloved cousin died of cancer. The memorial speeches were done, and the family stepped off to the side to chat. Hephzibah was identified by the Washington Attorney General. She has 14 out of 16 markers on facial recognition software. Hephzibah explained the situation she had at work with the man who was pro-ISIS. Hephzibah explained to her family and to the Attorney General, "I didn't want Youlin to break his family's streak of getting along equally well with both Jews and Muslims."

Hephzibah's sister, Julia, told her, "But they aren't really his family." Julia thought her sister was wrong about Youlin.

The Attorney General gently put her hand on Julia's arm and softly said, "You think you know what is going on, but you don't have it right."

"That's not the reason you were terminated," Hephzibah's mother said.

"Well, we don't know the reason I was terminated," Hephzibah responded.

"Why do you know the reason she was terminated," the Washington State Attorney General asked, "if she doesn't?" The Attorney General gave Hephzibah's mother a shrewd look.

[Clue #9 Intel contacted her mother to follow directions in the anonymous file.]

Hephzibah's mother said, "You were terminated for having an illicit relationship with Mike?"

Hephzibah responded, "First, I'll need to look up the word illicit in the dictionary. Second, I wasn't asked that. I was asked, 'Did you have a relationship with Mike or a Michael?' I was asked the question at work, by someone at work, about someone at work. So based on all context clues, I assumed this was about a work relationship." Hephzibah added, "I wasn't sure which Mike they were asking about. Mike is a common name." The first one named Michael was a character in *The Apocalypse of Zerubbabel*.

She considered that they might mean the archangel. Or possibly a technical writer for a magazine. The Mike at Intel was the last person to come to mind.

Hephzibah wasn't prepared for the urban dictionary version of the word "relationship." The person asking didn't explain and the man who wanted the question asked insisted it referred to something sexual without any context to indicate this. This was a cultural conflict.

Hephzibah's aunt asked, "She hadn't brought it up. She didn't know who you were talking about. So why did you ask the question?" Hephzibah's mother paused and gave her husband a suspicious look. Hephzibah's father lifted his gaze trying to remember.

[Clue #10 Names are getting confused. Clue #9 Intel using the anonymous file.]

The Washington Attorney General told Julia, "It is a bad attorney to take information as the situation, instead of a claim. You should have taken into consideration that your sister might be innocent." This Attorney General was not swayed by the anonymous complaint.

Hephzibah's mother said to Julia, "I'll tell them the information is wrong and that's been verified." She was intentionally mixing up the names and then claiming the information is already verified to discourage authorities from checking. "I have to say something," Hephzibah's mother said.

"No, you don't," Julia countered. "You really don't. This is what you've been doing all along!" Julia exclaimed. She told the family, "I'm being used to get her into trouble."

Hephzibah's parents hoped she would meet up with an ex in London. She hadn't informed her parents of the trip. Hephzibah entrusted Youlin with her London itinerary. Someone found a copy. Who?

[Clue #11 Someone was in her house.]

Her parents had wanted to marry her off to her ex. They thought it would be the best thing.

"Who is the ex?" she pressed. There was no answer. This situation was far from comforting.

[Clue #12 Parents are trying to pair her with an ex and won't say who the ex is.]

Putting all the clues together, it was suspected and later verified that Daniel was living in her garage and garden shed. This was a violation of the Protection Order. Daniel was prosecuted for the violation and taken in by the Federal Marshal on eight counts of murder. As more bodies are found, the number of murders is growing, and Daniel has more verified kills than any other person in American history. But that is another story, and actually a series of stories.

Her uncle said, "And to top this off, the emperor's grandson is real."

Hephzibah was unaware that her history report carried any significance. Under China's laws, this completely changes the history of China. But from her perspective, it didn't matter. Her concern was civil rights and a true republic with voting citizens.

 Hephzibah's mother pointed out, "Putting four candidates on the ballot and only allowing one choice is essentially defeating three rulers." This was a redeeming statement. If you tried to hit it, you would miss it. In this way, maybe Hephzibah was similar to the character in Zerubbabel's story.

The authorities intervened. The Education Division was surprised Hephzibah was so close to finishing her degree. They felt lied to. They checked her transcripts and found plenty of classes they could fill in for the missing class. "I thought she was parading a pregnancy," they said to the authorities, "not that she was trying to keep it secret." They added, "There are laws that protect a pregnancy." The matter is not yet fully resolved, but responsible parties at the university have been prosecuted and others were fired or resigned.

Hephzibah said, "I wanted to avoid the spectacle and the assumptions of the secretary." The Education Division took the request as accusing the math professor of fathering her pregnancy. "That doesn't make sense," Hephzibah objected. "The math professor's name isn't David."

They nodded. "Oh, I see," they said and paused, "The son of David doesn't mean it is a virgin birth. It means the father's name is David."

The Education Division asked Hephzibah about her king line, "How would you know?" Hephzibah explained the documentation and the professional genealogy study. This is the study Youlin paid for. She explained the DNA genomes, which show up because the line is repeated many times. They assumed family members had told her instead of paid research and DNA tests. "I see," they said to the local police, "She is too old to get that from a family member."

It wasn't hearsay. The genealogy was backed up by documentation and blood tests.

The Essential Documents

Youlin was sitting and reading this book. When he came to page 49, he stood to his feet. Youlin's father had lived his entire life without his birth certificate. He told Hephzibah, "Just write that the birth certificate is missing. That is what we tell people." He hadn't expected her to find the location of the essential documents.

Youlin called his mother to go to the Hong Kong and Shanghai Bank (HSBC) in Beijing, China.

Youlin's mother avoided the busiest time of the day. She arrived at the bank in her best clothing. She glanced over her left shoulder and hoped for privacy. She was much younger than Youlin's father, but her face was aged with worry.

There was an unavoidable smell of sweat as businessmen moved in and out of the bank. A businesswoman walked by with an armful of folders. She was wearing high heels. The floor was designed to muffle the sound of footsteps, and this gave the effect of disembodied suits moving throughout the building.

Youlin's mother sat in an empty chair to meet with a bank manager. She explained that her husband recently died, and his birth certificate was in a safe deposit box in their bank. The documents were placed in the safe by Sir Reginald Johnston on November 2, 1924, one year after her husband's birth.

The bank managers were skeptical of the widow, but they promised confidentiality. They planned to meet again to allow the bank to research the location of the safe and investigate the contents. It is a common occurrence for safes this old to need to be retrieved by a next of kin. They had a procedure to follow.

She called Youlin to intervene. "They are looking at me funny," she expressed. "Could you meet with them?"

"Sure," Youlin answered. He apologized to her for putting her through that. It must have been embarrassing. Soon after he spoke with the bank managers and explained the situation. The genealogy was proven by Pu Yi in Chinese court when his attorneys were on retainer. DNA evidence was submitted at that time and proved the paternity of the infant child. Youlin assured that recent DNA evidence could be provided if necessary.

The meeting paved the way for a smoother visit when Youlin's mother returned to the bank. The managers were cheerful, friendly, and respectful. The exchange was a relief.

The bank managers verified that the contents of the safe deposit box had remained untouched for nearly one hundred years. They could not be forgeries. There was no opportunity for tampering. The documents in the safe needed to be used as proof of next of kin. No other documents existed. They already had DNA evidence to show their genealogy.

I wrote another song, 1, 4, 5 in the key of B.

SALT OF THE EARTH

We are the salt of the earth,
Co-creators in beauty with our birth
God is the artist. We are his brush,
Transforming a barren desert to lush

We never see the results from above
Seasoned with salt and tempered in the son.

His design, part of His plan
His sandals of peace and the touch of His hand
Like grain in the desert replanted by birds.
We plant God's seeds using the Living Word.

We never see the result from above
Seasoned with salt and tempered in the son.

Add salt to the oil. Reduce the flashpoint.
Quiet the anger and see their viewpoint.
With pure motive, our piece.
Be preservatives yourselves. Preserve the peace.

He knows the result from above,
Seasoned with salt and tempered in the son.

At this revision, Israel is at war. Saed was caught sending money to
Hamas. Our government told me, "You won't have to worry about him
anymore."
The descendants of Jokshan are fighting the descendants of Israel. It is
Keturah versus Sarah. The prophet Mohammad, the founder of Islam, said
he was a descendant of Abraham through "the second wife and the second
son." The prophet spoke truth. There is a line to Sheba, son of Jokshan, son
of Keturah, Abraham's legal wife.

www.ingramcontent.com/pod-product-compliance
Lightning Source LLC
LaVergne TN
LVHW051130080426
835510LV00018B/2330